Democracy without Enemies

Democracy without Enemies

ULRICH BECK

Translated by Mark Ritter

Polity Press

Copyright © this collection Polity Press 1998
For further copyright details, please see acknowledgements page.
Published with the financial support of Inter Nationes, Bonn.
First published in 1998 by Polity Press in association with
Blackwell Publishers Ltd.

2 4 6 8 10 9 7 5 3 1

Editorial office:
Polity Press
65 Bridge Street
Cambridge CB2 1UR, UK

Marketing and production:
Blackwell Publishers Ltd
108 Cowley Road
Oxford OX4 1JF, UK

Published in the USA by
Blackwell Publishers Inc.
Commerce Place
350 Main Street
Malden, MA 02148, USA

A catalogue record for this book is available from the British Library.

Library of Congress Cataloging-in-Publication Data

Beck, Ulrich, 1944–
    Democracy without enemies / Ulrich Beck : translated by Mark
Ritter.
        p.   cm.
    Essays from various German language sources
    Includes bibliographical references and index.
    ISBN 0–7456–1822–7 (alk. paper). — ISBN 0–7456–1823–5 (pbk. :
alk. paper)
    1. Democracy.   2. Civilization, Modern.   3. Civil society.
I. Title.
JC423.B297   1998
321.8′09′049—dc21   98–6186
                                                                                               CIP

Typeset in 10 on 12 pt Sabon
by Graphicraft Typesetters Ltd., Hong Kong
Printed in Great Britain by TJ International, Padstow, Cornwall

This book is printed on acid-free paper.

Contents

Acknowledgements

The author and publishers wish to thank the following for permission to use copyright material: Philipp Reclam Jun. GmbH & Co. for the original German of chapters 3, 4, 8, 9, 11, 12; Süddeutscher Verlag GmbH for the original German of chapter 13; Suhrkamp Verlag for the original German of chapters 1, 2, 6, 7; *Dissent* for the English translation of chapter 5; Humanities Press, Inc. for the English translation of chapter 2, © 1995 Humanities International, Inc.; Siobhan Kattago for the English translation of chapter 10.

English translation of chapters 1, 3, 4, 6, 7, 8, 9, 11, 12, 13 and translation revisions in chapter 10 all copyright © 1998 Polity Press.

The chapters of the book were formerly published as follows (all essays translated by Mark Ritter unless indicated otherwise):

Chapter 1 as 'Kinder der Freiheit' in Ulrich Beck (ed.), *Kinder der Freiheit*, Suhrkamp, 1997.

Chapter 2 as 'Der Konflikt der zwei Modernen' in Ulrich Beck, *Politik in der Risikogesellschaft*, Suhrkamp, 1991. Translated by Mark Ritter in *Ecological Enlightenment: Essays on the Politics of the Risk Society*, Humanities Press, 1995.

Chapter 3 as 'Vom Verschwinden der Solidarität' in Ulrich Beck, *Die feindlose Demokratie: Ausgewählte Aufsätze*, Reclam, 1995.

Chapter 4 as 'Perspektiven einer kulturellen Evolution der Arbeit' in Ulrich Beck, *Die feindlose Demokratie: Ausgewählte Aufsätze*, Reclam, 1995.

Chapter 5 as 'Kapitalismus ohne Arbeit' in *Der Spiegel*, no. 20 (1996), pp. 140–6. Translated by Krishna Winston in *Dissent* (Winter 1997), pp. 51–6.

Chapter 6 as 'Demokratisierung der Familie' in Ulrich Beck (ed.), *Kinder der Freiheit*, Suhrkamp, 1997.

Chapter 7 as 'Wissen oder Nicht-Wissen' in Ulrich Beck, Anthony Giddens and Scott Lash, *Reflexive Modernisierung*, Suhrkamp, 1996.

Chapter 8 as 'Renaissance des Politischen' in Ulrich Beck, *Die feindlose Demokratie*, Reclam, 1995.

Chapter 9 as 'Die Offene Stadt' in Ulrich Beck, *Die feindlose Demokratie*, Reclam, 1995.

Chapter 10 as 'Wie aus Nachbarn Juden werden' in Ulrich Beck, *Die feindlose Demokratie*, Reclam, 1995. Translated by Siobhan Kattago in *Constellations*, vol. 2, no. 3 (Jan. 1996). Translation revised by Mark Ritter for this edition.

Chapter 11 as 'Der feindlose Staat' in Ulrich Beck, *Die feindlose Demokratie*, Reclam, 1995.

Chapter 12 as 'Kleine Anleitung zum ökologischen Machiavellismus' in Ulrich Beck, *Die feindlose Demokratie*, Reclam, 1995.

Chapter 13 as 'Die Utopie der Selbstbegrenzung', *Süddeutsche Zeitung*, 17 May 1995.

1

Freedom's Children

The Berlin Wall has collapsed. But a chorus of criticism is shaking and blocking the West. Are we a society of egoists? One might almost think so if one reviewed the slogans echoing through the public sphere: the dissolving of solidarity, the decline of values, the culture of narcissism, the egoism trap, entitlement thinking, hedonism. Franz Kamphaus, the Catholic Bishop of Limburg, Germany, writes:

> Every moment on the infinite playing field of freedom is accompanied by crises of relationships, the renunciation of loyalties and cracks in the chain of tradition. Does a person who wants to live out his freedom ultimately only live out himself? Will modern societies fail from their atomization, their exhaustion of solidarity?[1]

The enemy stereotypes of the East–West conflict are relinquished and replaced by the diagnosis of neo-Spenglerism that solidarity is exhausted. The environmental crisis comes to mind here. Modern society lives from natural resources that it has consumed and destroyed, but also from moral resources, which it is equally unable to renew. The transcendental 'values ecology', in which communalism, solidarity, justice and ultimately democracy are 'rooted', is decaying.

In contrast to that, the sceptic of democracy, Alexis de Tocqueville, wrote as long ago as 1848 that 'fighting against freedom means fighting against God himself' (Tocqueville 1945). What might that wanderer between the worlds of the feudal and democratic ages have meant by this? A self-authorization of the individual was characteristic of European modernity from the very beginning. Its origin does not lie in capitalism, not even in humanism and certainly not in the 'death of God' (Nietzsche), but in the world of changing religious experiences of ancient Judaism and early Christianity, as well as in the discovery and the release of the power of reason in Greek philosophy.

A few chapters later in de Tocqueville's *Democracy in America*, one finds this sentence, which is hardly less shocking to many people today: 'The Americans battled individualism, the fruit of equality, with freedom, and they have vanquished it' (1945: 591). Applied to the present debate, this implies that the symptoms of the 'me generation' cannot be opposed with less freedom; they must be opposed with more freedom, but *political* freedom. Freedom, if seized and actively filled out, fosters commitments in the public space and is thus the exact opposite of the neoliberal idolization of the market.

This prescription, opposing decline with public freedom, is so important because it is in such dramatic opposition to the view almost dominant today that modernity needs, indeed uses up, ties (Dahrendorf's 'ligatures') which it cannot itself renew. In this conception, modernity is inherently counterproductive. It permanently undermines its indispensable moral prerequisites. This self-concept of modern society (and its philosophy and sociology) is completely false. Christianity and political freedom are not mutually exclusive, but mutually inclusive, even if this builds an insoluble contradiction into the Christian traditions.

The point is to give a simple, comprehensible answer to a complicated question. The question is: what is modernity? The answer is: not just 'instrumental rationality' (Max Weber), 'optimal use of capital' (Karl Marx) or 'functional differentiation' (Talcott Parsons, Niklas Luhmann), but supplementing and conflicting with these, it is *political freedom*, citizenship and civil society. The point of this answer is that meaning, morality and justice are not preordained and, as it were, extraterritorial variables for modern society. Quite the reverse is true. Modernity has an independent, living and simultaneously ancient and highly up-to-date well-spring of meaning in its midst: political freedom.[2] The latter is not exhausted by daily use; instead, it bubbles up with greater life and vigour. Modernity accordingly means that a world of traditional certainty is perishing and being replaced, if we are fortunate, by legally sanctioned individualism for everyone.

Just stay at home: young people practise a highly political disavowal of politics

We Western Europeans are not living in a crisis of culture, and certainly not in a decline of values; instead, we are threatened by something much 'worse'. Our words of freedom are beginning to become deeds in everyday life and are thus calling into question the bases of our previous coexistence, which relied on the precondition that we would only talk of political freedom, not act according to it. The 'catastrophe' is therefore that we must understand, acknowledge and put up with more and different types of freedom than those foreseen in the picture book of democracy as spoken of and promised, but not lived up to. Being freedom's children thus means that we are living under the preconditions of *internalized* democracy, for which many of the concepts and formulas of primary modernity have become inadequate.

No one knows how the traditional authority structure of the family can be connected to the new demands for freedom and self-realization for men and women. The high divorce rates and the figures on single-person households all speak this language.

No one knows how individualism and Christian faith can be reharmonized. And yet sociologists demonstrate that, along with individualization, the willingness to exist for others, indeed to believe, is growing and not disappearing.[3] No one knows how the needs of mass organizations (political parties and trade unions, but cities and communities as well) to obligate the individual are compatible with claims for self-participation and self-organization. No one knows how this immense variety can be mobilized and concentrated for politically necessary decisions.

We are therefore 'suffering' from freedom and not from a crisis. More precisely, we are suffering from the unintended consequences and expressions of a now customary increase in freedom, which was invoked at least on the level of lip service. Kant and Hegel were the first in Germany to set foot firmly in the land of modernity. We owe them the insight that even 'concretizing freedom' is a revolution, albeit a quiet one, occurring because the foundations of the previous social order must be renegotiated.[4]

If this interpretation can be supported, then the talk of a 'decline of values' contains something else, namely the fear of freedom, including the fear of freedom's children, who must struggle with new and different types of problems raised by *internalized* freedom. How can the longing for self-determination be brought into harmony with the equally important longing for shared community? How can one simultaneously be individualistic and merge with the group? How might the variety of voices which vie within each of us in a confusing world be combined into a political statement and action pointing beyond the present day?[5]

The spaces in which people think and act in a morally responsible manner are becoming, on the one hand, smaller and more intensive in that they comprise one's own immediate surroundings, and here the demands increase to the point where they cannot be fulfilled. On the other hand, they are becoming more voluminous and difficult to manage, even immune to any action at all. Young people are moved by that which (established) politics largely rules out: how can global environmental destruction be resolved? How can the death of hope signified by unemployment, a threat to prosperity's children, be prevented and overcome? How can one love and live, with the threat of AIDS? All these are questions that slip through the screens of the large political organizations. The consequence is that freedom's children practise a highly political disavowal of politicians.

They hate organizations for their formalism and their convoluted and dishonest call for 'selfless' commitment, and they practise the kind of voting with their feet that was so profoundly underestimated some time ago by the leaders of East Germany. They simply stay at home. The members of Britain's Conservative Party have already reached a very venerable average age of over 60. One of these days, people in Germany will also have to face up to the question of whether grandpa's mega-organizations will really be justified in their lament over the 'decline of values' when the last member resigns.

Those who want to get involved go to Greenpeace. According to a survey of the German Youth Institute, more than 60 per cent of young people consider the environmental activists credible. The parties, on the other hand, rank right at the bottom of the scale in the same survey, in eighth place, well behind trade unions, the press and the church. The scepticism of young people applies to parties of all stripes. While 6.8 per cent of the members of the (conservative) Christian Democratic Union were under 30 years old in 1991, the same group accounted for only 4.9 per cent in 1995. In the same period, the average age of CDU members rose by two to nearly 54. The typical Social Democrat does not look much younger. He too has almost half a century behind him. Only 7.4 per cent of his comrades are under 30. The (middle of the road) Free Democratic Party is also losing more and more of its younger generation. Its youth group has lost more than 2,000 members since 1991.

All parties are suffering because the me generation may participate in demonstrations and in circulating petitions, but it finds the business of organized politics, with its debates on agendas and proposals, intensely boring. 'The loyal party soldier, who first pastes up posters for years and finally manages to make it into the town council, is a dying species,' says social researcher Helmut Jung.[6]

Young people have finally discovered something for themselves, something to make adults panic: fun, fun sports, fun music, fun consumption, fun life. But politics, as currently practised and represented, has nothing at all to do with fun. On the contrary, it acts like a dead-certain killjoy, and hence young people are unpolitical, according to superficial impressions and in their own understanding, but in a very political way. Freedom's children regroup in a colourful rebellion against tedium and obligations that are to be complied with without reasons being given for them and even if no one can identify with them.

Thus there is a subterranean connection between wanting to have fun and grass-roots opposition, which has so far been little noticed but which constitutes the actual core of what one could call the 'politics of youthful antipolitics'. Those who (whatever their intentions) refuse to care about institutionalized politics (parties, organizations, etc.), but playfully follow the attractions of, for instance, advertising, are unintentionally acting very politically by depriving politics of attention, labour, consent and power. Ultimately, one can spare oneself the detour through membership meetings and enjoy the blessings of political action by heading straight to the disco. There is no need to raise the issue of power long-windedly by actual attendance. It gets raised, and more effectively so, the more decisively, mutely and numerously young people simply stay away.[7]

Freedom's children sometimes betray a winking awareness of this subliminally very effective connection, its subversive energy and irony, which would be more at home and better expressed in the art of the novel than in sociology. Everyone, the elite of the institutions as well as the young people, seems to sense that this policy of conforming withdrawal calls the system into question, once it is practised consistently enough.

This is how and where freedom's children display an unarticulated 'double strategy'. They are an actively unpolitical younger generation because they take the life out of the self-involved institutions and thus force upon them the Hamlet question: to be or not to be? This Western variant of 'antipolitics' (György Konrad), which also opens up the opportunity to enjoy one's own life with the best conscience in the world, is supplemented and made credible by a self-organized concern for others which has broken free from large institutions. Freedom's children practise a seeking, experimenting morality that ties together things that seem mutually exclusive: egoism *and* altruism, self-realization *and* active compassion, self-realization *as* active compassion. Ultimately this amounts to questioning the monopoly of the custodians of the public interest on defining the public interest.

Robert Wuthnow (1997) shows that all modern societies would collapse without voluntary activities for others (see also Wilkinson 1997). Eighty million Americans, roughly 45 per cent of those above the age of 18, are involved for five or more hours a week in voluntary service for charitable purposes. In monetary terms this amounts to some 150 billion dollars.

The astonishing thing is this: for more than 75 per cent of the American population, solidarity, willingness to help others and concern for the public interest have a prominence equal to such motivations as self-realization, occupational success and the expansion of personal freedom. The real surprise is that self-assertion, enjoying oneself *and* caring for others are not mutually exclusive; they are mutually inclusive and strengthen and enrich one another. Insight into this seemingly paradoxical situation is blocked by four prevailing fundamental assumptions in public and scholarly debate:

1　The equation and confusion of commitment with *membership* – if membership lists are the only things that show commitment, then non-members are of necessity egotists;

2　The self-sacrifice assumption, that only by ignoring oneself can one live for others;

3　Silent help or the *housewife syndrome*, conveying that the dignity of serving others is that it remains invisible, that is, unpaid and unacknowledged, done at the behest of others who are in control;

4　A clear separation of roles between helpers and needy – it never occurs to anyone that those who commit themselves to others also need help and *receive* it from their service, that perhaps the enrichment might lie precisely in the experience of mutual helplessness.

If one puts together these four assumptions of the equation of commitment and membership, the principles of selflessness and invisibility and the image of the heroic helper-and-nothing-but, then one has (albeit in a rather crude distortion) the intimidating image that forces freedom's children to *flee* organizations. The latter equate commitment with selflessly performed service. Accordingly, the individual becomes anonymous in hierarchical dependency, a foot soldier in a 'public interest army', a mere executing agent in predetermined 'sacrificial' cases.[8]

The much maligned decline of values is generating new value orientations for the second modernity

At heart, we are thus concerned not with a decline of values but with a *conflict* of values, with two images of society, politics and democracy which are different in style and content. Those who lament the decline of values are very much up on their high horses as they complain about the 'ungrateful society' and the ungrateful younger generation who are simply unwilling to recognize how well our institutions (and those who control them) are managing everything.

Many young people (one must be very careful with generalizations, because these are freedom's children, after all) find themselves confronting completely changed global situations and problems, on both the large and the small scale, in their own life milieu and in global society. The adults and the institutions they direct have no answer to these because they have never experienced them and do not take them seriously. Freedom's children 'find they face a world that no longer falls into two camps, but rather into a vast group of fracture lines, cracks and gaps among which no one any longer knows the way. The future has become multidimensional; the patterns of explanation offered by older people are no longer effective. . . . There are many more riddles than solutions and even the solutions, looked at more closely, prove to be sacks full of riddles.'[9]

The danger of the new diversity is not the alleged confusion it brings. It lies in the inability of political parties, trade unions, churches, organizations and so on to deal with this increased diversity. Those in charge must give themselves a kick in the pants: stop demonizing individualism, which has already become a reality, and instead acknowledge it as a desirable and inevitable product of democratic evolution. They should realize that this is an expression of the Western heritage. Only then can one convincingly ask what political orientations and degree of accommodation are emerging in the individualized and globalized society of the second modernity.

What astonishes and angers me is that the conservative wailing about the alleged decline of values is not only completely false, it also obstructs the view of precisely the sources and movements from which can be created a readiness to take on the tasks of the future. The much demonized decline of values actually *produces* the orientations and prerequisites which, if anything can, will put this society in a position to master the future.

The basic idea is that without the expansion and strengthening of political freedom and its social form, civil society, nothing will work in the future. In this regard, it is important first of all to recognize that changing values and acceptance of democracy go hand in hand. An inner kinship exists between the values of self-development and the ideal of democracy. Many of the findings that research into the changes in values has brought to light, such as the spontaneity and voluntarism of political activism, self-organization, the resistance to formalism and hierarchies, contrariness, tentativeness, as well as the reservation of getting involved only where one can remain in control of the activity, may indeed collide with the party apparatus, but they certainly make sense in the forms and forums of civil society.

One can elaborate this in relation to a number of challenges. The major figures in the study of values (Helmut Klages and Ronald Inglehart,

Gerhard Schmidtchen, Daniel Yankelovich, Robert Wuthnow and Helen Wilkinson) all agree that the change in attitudes does *not* amount to an inflation of material demands. On the contrary, the old and apparently eternal pattern of 'more income, more consumption, more career, more conspicuous consumption' is breaking up and being replaced by a new weighting of priorities, which may often be difficult to decipher, but in which immaterial factors of the quality of life play an outstanding part. What does this imply? For one thing, control over a person's 'own time' is valued higher than more income and more career success, because time is the key that opens the door to the treasures promised by the age of self-determined life: dialogue, friendship, being on one's own, compassion, fun and so on.

This means that the struggle over the distribution of material goods, which still monopolizes public and social scientific attention, has been undermined for some time by a struggle over the distribution of scarce immaterial goods that can hardly be offset by (expressed in) money, such as rest, leisure, self-determined commitments, the love of adventure, interchanges with others and so forth. In the endangered ways of life of our highly civilized world, these are gaining urgency and attractiveness.

In the age of the self-determined life, the social perception of what constitutes 'wealth' and 'poverty' is changing so radically that, under certain conditions, less income and status, if they go hand in hand with the opportunity for more self-development and more ability to arrange things personally, may be perceived as an advance and not a setback. This should not be celebrated without reservation, since it is certainly the underlying cultural perception explaining why the dramatic exacerbation of material social inequality has . . . so far! . . . been accepted without a political outcry. Conversely, however, this shows an unexpected opportunity to turn less into more: material sacrifices are tolerable if they go hand in hand with a guaranteed increase of self-developed society. A freedom society, not a leisure society, could perhaps allow us to say good-bye to growth-oriented labour society.[10]

People are better adapted to the future than are social institutions and their representatives. It is important to recognize that the secular change also creates the preconditions for mastering it, but preconditions (and only partial ones at that), not a guarantee. The decline of values which cultural pessimists are so fond of decrying is in fact opening up the possibility of escaping from the creed of 'bigger, more, better' in a period that is living beyond its means ecologically and economically. It is particularly the apostles of the status quo who grumble that individualization means egocentrism; this expresses more about themselves than about those whom they claim to criticize. While in the old values system the ego always had to be subordinated to patterns of the collective (also always designed by individuals), these new orientations towards the 'we' create something like a *cooperative or altruistic individualism*.[11] Thinking of oneself and living for others at the same time, once considered a contradiction in terms, is revealed as an internal, substantive connection. Living alone means living socially.[12]

Research also shows that, in contrast to the distortion implied by the term 'dog-eat-dog society', tolerance for other types of people and marginal groups, whether foreigners, homosexuals, handicapped people or the socially disadvantaged, has steadily increased as values have changed (see Klages 1996). An epoch in which global society finds itself disturbingly refracted in personal life is finding in the alleged 'decline of values' precisely the willingness to appropriate external things which, as Georg Simmel shows, gives birth to the miracle of the new.

One final example: it is often asserted in gloomy tones that today's 'mobile people' have become devoid of commitments. A recent study of singles (not a group, but a category that comprises a number of very heterogeneous situations) shows that mobility is indeed highly valued. The idea of having to practise a 'lifetime profession' is considered a burden rather than something desirable, while change, in work as well as in relationships, is considered natural and desirable by many. Who could fail to recognize here that one core promise of modernity, mobility, is being turned against another, the ideal of a lifelong profession as internalized in primary modernity? No one is saying that this can occur painlessly and succeed without contradictions. One does not need to read tea leaves, however, to recognize that the structural transformation creates preferences that enhance the status of the imperative to deal with diversity and mobility.

Here too, one sees that the age of the self-determined life is not populated entirely by people demanding benefits, people quarrelling, making trouble, shirking. Quite the contrary, orientations and priorities come into being here that surreptitiously meet the challenges of the second modernity. Personal responsibility, self-organization and personal politics are getting an enlightened and realistic chance to redistribute responsibility and power in society, but this opportunity must now be seized by a politics that is hitting its limits in every respect.

The short-lived dream of everlasting prosperity

The poet Hölderlin may have believed that danger is the mother of salvation, but none of the rest of us should be swept away by such sentiments. For freedom's children encounter a world in which prosperity, once considered certain, is eroding. Even though some would like to deny it, it remains true that freedom presupposes security, as shown most impressively and emphatically by T. H. Marshall in his famous study on *Citizenship and Social Class*. Accordingly, the former prime minister of Spain, Felipe Gonzales, observes: 'Freedom is, generally speaking, not a primary striving of people, but something people seek when their other needs have been met . . . I believe that security is the primary emotion, so that we are closer to the instinct of animals . . . When security is lost, the sense of freedom becomes weak and fragile.'[13]

The faster and more thoroughly social transformation changes the operating principles of living, working and running a household, the more probable it is that people will feel overburdened and the more the *fear of freedom* will spread. Thus studies show that more and more people consider their life and well-being under threat, even though the number of violent crimes (in Germany) is not increasing, but stagnating at a relatively low level or even decreasing slightly. It is important to distinguish between crime and fear of crime, which does not feed on crime itself but on the general feeling of uncertainty (see Hitzler 1996).

'The more freedom we have, the more troublesome and threatening it seems,' writes Zygmunt Bauman (1996). 'I believe that people today are not so much concerned with the need to belong to a community as with liberation from the compulsion of constantly having to choose and decide.' Where freedom becomes a cage, many choose the freedom of a cage (new or old religious movements, fundamentalism, drugs or violence).[14]

How is one to understand this paradox of 'imposed freedom', which so many are seeking to escape? A self-determined life is not a self-chosen form of existence, but rather a structural principle based on the entire society and it can be influenced only to a limited extent. 'Programmed individualism' is the slogan, which becomes more comprehensible if one connects Kafka's world-view to that of Sartre. The age of the self-determined life is produced by a dense fabric of institutions (law, education, the labour market and so on) which 'condemn' everyone 'to freedom' (Sartre) on pain of (economic) disadvantage.[15]

The crucial point is that paid labour, the cornerstone that integrated people socially and materially into society, is eroding in the context of 'institutionalized individualism' (Parsons). Unemployment no longer threatens only marginal groups, but also the middle sections of society, even groups (such as doctors and executives) which, until a few years ago, were considered the very quintessence of middle-class economic security. Moreover, this is happening on such a massive scale that the difference between unemployment and threatening unemployment is becoming insignificant to the affected parties. To understand the extent of this transformation of the foundations of modern society ('reflexive modernization'), it makes sense to distinguish three phases of development since the Second World War.

For the first phase (extending into the 1960s) the necessity and obviousness of rebuilding a destroyed world meshed together with the fear that what had been achieved might again collapse, and consequently classical virtues such as willingness to sacrifice, diligence, self-denial, subordination and living for others mutually reinforced one another.

'The short-lived dream of eternal prosperity' (Burkart Lenz) could be the key phrase for the second phase, which reached into the 1980s. The earned wealth was considered certain; the 'side-effects' (the environmental crisis, individualization), which call the foundation of primary modernity into question, were repressed (by the established order) and brought to public awareness by varying protest movements. Political freedoms developed then and radiated out into the overall society.

In a third phase, which I have described as the 'global risk society', there is a return of uncertainty, which did not just shake public trust in the ability of key institutions of the industrial world, of business, law and politics, to tame and control the threatening effects they produce; there is also a sense that, across all income groups, prosperity biographies become risk biographies, losing their social identity and material faith in future security.

> Against the background of economic decline, the dominant fear is now that the prosperity once considered secure could collapse. People have lost their orientations and have reached the conclusion that it might make sense after all to think about the future. They worry about their chances in the labor market, the level of their income, the four walls around them, the education of their children and the security of their old-age pensions. (Yankelovich 1994)

When advanced capitalism in the highly developed countries breaks up the core values of work society, a historic alliance between capitalism, the welfare state and democracy shatters. Democracy arose in Europe and America as a 'democracy of work' in the sense that political freedom relied on participation in paid labour. The citizen had to earn a living one way or another in order to fill the political freedoms with life.

The consequence is that 'citizens mobilize more and more often and more and more self-confidently against rowdies of both right and left, against criminals, against disruptive and annoying elements, against drug dealers and hustlers; and against their own anxieties for the future,' writes

Ronald Hitzler (1996). A citizens' initiative movement for security and order appears to be succeeding the environmental, women's and peace movements and setting off on its own 'march through the institutions'. Here, conversely, the risks of freedom, that is, of liberality and the decline of standards, are denounced and self-help and other remedies are being put into practice.

We have to shout to be heard by neoliberals worldwide, given their ignorance of historical experience: the market fundamentalism they worship is a form of democratic illiteracy. The market does *not* have an inherent justification. This economic model is capable of surviving only in an interplay of material security, social-welfare rights and democracy. Counting only on the market implies destroying democracy along with the economic mode.

Emphasizing this publicly is one thing, but opening people's eyes to the realities is something quite different. Large and growing groups of the populace are excluded *inside* modernity from the prerequisites for making a living and the safety nets of modernity. The crucial point is not only that radical collapses and splits are occurring or impending, but that these are brought about against the background of *fully established* modernity as a 'modernization of modern society'. The key issue is therefore: how do self-confident citizens who are aware of their freedoms react when they see the security of their world tottering and see themselves subject to radical inequalities?

In this third phase in the 1990s, cutbacks of fundamental rights, fear of the future and demands for and awareness of freedom coincide. This is the constellation that gives birth to the *ugly citizen* (see Beck 1998). Where it is necessary to put up with threatened or lost social security in a milieu of perceived political freedom, civic virtues turn ugly and aggressive.

The face of the second modernity will therefore not resemble the ideal image of the citizen in all his or her kindness and beauty. Instead, it will be necessary to bid farewell to wide-eyed hopes for an ideal marriage of self-organization and reason, not out of some culturally pessimistic sense of inevitable failure, but as an ever-present possibility. This loses its terror when one sees that precisely the abuse of freedom is freedom's most reliable indicator.

Anyone who would like to know how free a country and its people are should not look only at the constitution and should leave debates in parliament and governmental programmes aside. Instead, attention should be paid to how people behave with respect to excesses of freedom (pornography, criminality by 'foreigners', violence among young people); if they react with composure, then freedom is in good hands.

It is a simple statement, but none the less true: freedom also has an ugly side. This is not a refutation, but a proof of freedom, of its really human, that is to say fallible, dimension.

Political responses: neoliberalism, communitarianism and cosmopolitan republicanism

What political responses are struggling with one another here? To mention just the keywords: neoliberalism, communitarianism, protectionism.

The *neoliberals* of the world have most clearly gathered their ranks under the banner of the *market* and are rehearsing an attack on the crumbling foundations of primary modernity, such as the welfare state, the nation-state, trade union power or 'ecological inhibitions on private investment'. The consequences are fatal for the individual as well as society, because an antihuman image of humanity is being elevated here to the status of a foundation for social intercourse. Social exclusion becomes the rule. Success in the market ultimately decides existence or non-existence. Consequently, adaptation becomes the highest goal of character formation. The political concept of society fades or disappears.[16]

The French sociologist Pierre Bourdieu recommends that anyone professing allegiance to neoliberalism be set down by helicopter in the ghettos of the outcasts in North and South American cities. He is certain that, after at most a week, such a person would come back as a convert to the welfare state.

The opponents of the neoliberals, the *communitarians*, march against the flag of the market with that of the *community*, and most powerfully, interestingly enough, in those countries where neoliberalism has raged the longest and most devastatingly, namely the USA and Great Britain. Markets and contracts, according to the intellectual code here, do not create any social cohesion in and of themselves. They require and use up the active identification of citizens with their communities as 'social mortar'. In that sense, the communitarian movement can be understood only as a movement in opposition to the 'neoliberalism of greed'. But while the new idolizers of the market *act*, and very effectively at that, the communitarians are satisfied in essence with *cosmetic measures*. They are attempting in the final analysis to exorcize the evil of egoism with a sanctimonious rhetoric of community spirit, a home remedy from grandma's medicine cabinet which, as we know, costs nothing and is worth every penny.

Many communitarians confuse moralizing with analysing. They forget that there is not just the danger of too little community, but that of too much as well, as the history of Germany in this century notably attests. The German-born American historian Albert O. Hirschman writes:

> During the Weimar Republic there was often complaining in Germany about the lack of certain social qualities that a society was supposed to have according to the understanding of the times. A sense of mission, a feeling of belonging together and a certain warmth – in short, community spirit – were missed. The Nazi movement owed its success in no small part to its promise to satisfy these alleged 'needs' in abundance by creating a newly strengthened *Volksgemeinschaft*.[17]

The majority of the communitarians take the existing institutions as a constant and thus misunderstand that these are being changed down to their very foundations by reflexive modernization (see Beck 1996; Beck, Giddens and Lash 1994).

The (still) silent majority of *protectionists* is meandering aimlessly in the no-man's-land between the neoliberals and the communitarians. Despite widely varying political objectives, the protectionists are united in the attempt to defend the old world-view and order of battle intellectually and politically against the onslaught of the realities of the second modernity. Beneath the surface layer of agitated debates on globalization, an all-party coalition of protectionism is forming. The conservative protectionists bemoan the decline of values and the loss of significance of the national. The left-wing protectionists are shaking the dust out of the old costumes from the class struggle just in case they might be needed. The green protectionists are discovering the charms of the nation-state and its range of weapons for defending environmental standards against the encroachment of the global market.

The irony is that Germany, occupied with itself and the problems of unifying West with East Germany, has thus far largely slept through these warring solutions: neoliberalism, communitarianism and protectionism. Rather than hopping on to a train that other countries are already leaving, it could therefore now tie together opposing movements, articulate them and convert them into practical politics. I would like to call this continental European position the cultural policy of a *cosmopolitan republicanism* and characterize it by five principles.

First is the new significance of the *individual*, with whom the right and the left, all varieties of communitarianism and the environmental movement have such difficulties. Second is the centrality of *cosmopolitan* agents, identities, networks and institutions. Third (and only apparently contradicting this) is the new significance of the *local*, the magic of place in world society. The two latter aspects run deeply against the grain of those who view the national and the nation-state as the *non plus ultra* of (primary) modernity. Fourth, there is the crucial significance of *political freedom*, that is, an active civil society, for the cohesion and self-responsibility of democracy beyond labour society, as well as for how it might become possible to respond to the ecological crisis. Fifth is the concluding insight that derives from all of this, the necessity for deep-seated *institutional reforms*, indeed a reformation of primary industrial modernity that would affirm diversity and 'cultivated conflict' (Helmut Dubiel). A few explanations of these points will be given using the example of municipal politics.

The redefinition of the local in the age of globalization

In the late 1930s, two Jewish émigrés in Paris are discussing their plans. One wants to emigrate to Uruguay. 'So far away?' asks the other in astonishment. 'Far away from where?' the first man replies. The fate of the rootless, the homeless and the stateless bursts forth in this question, as Hannah Arendt has depicted so incisively. Especially in global society, the citizen needs an (imaginary) place. But the problem of what that means is now coming up again, since place must be defined directly and autonomously in global society, while the national framework loses its significance (see Albrow 1996a).

'City' and 'citizenship' have more than just an etymological kinship. Civil society and political freedom have their social origin and their locus in a tangible local area. Strengthening civil society therefore implies strengthening local politics and identity, strengthening cities against the national centres. Large cities can no longer be just destinations in a shunting yard of the great problems. Everyone shifts everything imaginable and unimaginable on to cities and there is even a lovely word for it: the mature citizen.

The revaluation of the local as a response to globalization will therefore not be possible without reform of, for instance, municipal finances, and a revised distribution of power and problems between national and local politics. Are there models and conceptual targets for this in political philosophy and theory? Indeed there are.

If one asks us Germans for our admission ticket to the democratic age, we do not have a French, an American or even an English revolution to show off, but we do have Immanuel Kant. Our revolution occurred in the realm of thought, bears the noble name of *Critique of Pure Reason* and can gather dust in bookshelves. If one blows away the dust and begins to read, one notes with some displeasure that, to put it ironically, Kant, our officially licensed philosophical revolutionary, was outside the boundaries of our constitution. He took on himself the freedom to label

parliamentary democracy 'despotic', because the principle of representation contradicts the self-determination of the individual. 'Among the
three forms of the state, democracy, in the strict sense of the word, is
necessarily a despotism,' because it is the foundation for an executive
power in which '*all*, who indeed are *not all*, *decide* against one who
agrees or dissents, which is a contradiction of the general will with itself
and with freedom.'[18] This is the German way of revolution led by its
'purest reason'.

I consider this contrast between national majority democracy and a
cosmopolitan republicanism of the local to be one of the crucial themes
being placed on the agenda in the transition to the second modernity by
a grand coalition of necessity and reason. The shrinking labour society,
the overburdened and unaffordable welfare state, but also the terrible
efforts, in the truest sense of the word, that are demanded of us all to
alleviate the ecological crisis in that new focus of globalization, all of
these overtax the nation-state and institutionalized politics based on it.
How then can the political system – parliament, parties, government –
be unburdened and how can the self-responsibility of civil society be supported and expanded? How can these two sites and regulative agencies of
politics share the load of future problems and power and still be attuned
to one another? No one will be able to avoid this question. The answer
is: only by upgrading the local area of democracy, the towns and cities.

All of this presumes, among many other things, a repoliticization of
municipal policy, indeed a rediscovery and redefinition of it by mobilizing programmes, ideas and people to make the incomprehensible and
impossible real and possible, step by step.[19]

I am afraid that civil society is in such poor repute among politicians
partly because it does not meet the efficiency standards of a professional
politician. A rational-democratic self-misunderstanding of politics lies
concealed here and must finally be expressed. Politics must not be merely
rational in a democratic society, it must also be emotional. Efficient solutions are important, but so are passions, the ability to listen, justice, interests, trust, identities, and conflict when necessary; these involve, moreover,
materials that are objectively so complex that the concept of the single
optimal path which still haunts so many minds is completely illusory.

Politics is language, language is politics. Someone who wishes to
inspire must speak inspiringly. This reveals a close relationship between
art and politics. Language is what has remained for us. *Community spirit*,
which many obviously miss so painfully, is formed only in the symbols
created and reaffirmed in public speaking and listening. That is why the
technocratic plastic speech of so many politicians is a cancer on democratic culture. Language is the site and the medium for creating and caring

for the social sphere. We live in language. And who would care to live in the utterances of politicians? Not even politicians themselves, I fear.

Like so many other things, it has become unclear what really constitutes a 'city'. The criteria for creating an identity, such as a river, a group of historic buildings, the seat of government, a cathedral or other features that refer to a specific geographical point, have lost meaning because of the intensification of mobility, travel and information. Even cities can no longer rest in the security of a firmly emplaced geographical identity. They must be reinvented, as it were. Inventing does not mean designing on a draftsman's table; the public image of a city, its identity, which determines so many other things, must instead be created, shaped and coloured as a magic intoxicated with and tested by reality. Municipal politicians, at least the good ones, are urban magicians who shape the identity of their city, in competition with others, by public stage management, the development of urban projects and urban architecture.

What is considered an attractive and identity-fostering symbol in this regard is by no means arbitrary. An opera house might work, but not a six-lane multilevel highway intersection or a radio tower with a revolving restaurant on top. Low crime rates might be useful, but they do not create magic in and of themselves. A nuclear fusion reactor for research purposes that provokes international mistrust would probably also have the opposite of the intended effect. On the other hand, exemplary solutions to urban problems are certainly capable of developing such a magical attraction. One need only think of the idea of a zero-emission industrial park, in which factories are so interlocked that one reuses the wastes of another, as has been done in the United States. In this way, the frog no one wanted to kiss turns into a sought-after prince.

On curiosity about the unknown society in which we are living

Two epochal processes above all others, individualization and globalization, are changing the foundations of living together in all spheres of social action.[20] Both only superficially appear to be threats; they force but they also permit society to prepare and reshape itself for a second modernity. People are not to blame for the immobility; indeed it is essential to recognize that cultural individualization and globalization create precisely that historical orientation and those preconditions for an adaptation of institutions to a coming second modernity that are obstructed by the institutions (or those controlling them). The problem is obstacles in perception. Thinking has to change.

The conservative bemoaning of the decline of values (in all social camps) is not only self-righteous, it is also stricken with historical and empirical blindness. In Germany we have managed to put two dictatorships behind us, both of which stood under the motto: 'you are nothing, your class is everything.' Against this background, the amount of individualization that has been achieved is a decided advance. This is all the more true since it is completely false to equate individualization with unpolitical behaviour, indifference and egoism. Instead, the conceptions of what is political and what is not are changing. We are dealing with 'freedom's children', for whom the traditional patent remedies for living together (in marriage, parenthood, family, class and nation) have lost their practicability.

The two key concepts that characterize the situation after the collapse of the East–West enemy stereotype in what is now 'democracy without enemies' are *ambivalence* and *vacuum*. *Ambivalence* designates the simultaneity of relief and fear, initiative and fear. The loss of clarity is the paralysing thing, intellectually and politically. In quite superficial terms, there has never been such a remarkable increase in the number of liberal democracies, in the East but also in the south of the world. It is too quickly forgotten that a thoroughly militarized system of orthodox communism imploded *peacefully*. At the same time, however, nationalism, wars and civil wars have re-erupted everywhere. In Europe, the madness of 'ethnic cleansing' is winning victories and founding states. Even dyed-in-the-wool pacifists find themselves forced to reconsider the connection of freedom, human rights and war. Is there a right or a duty to go to war when human rights are being barbarically violated? Where does this have a limit? In Europe? Are genocides in Africa and Asia in the blind spot of this new 'global domestic policy'? Will we have to choose in the future between two unbearable alternatives, shocking indifference or global wars for human rights?

Vacuum means that even the victorious institutions of the West, NATO, the free market, the welfare state, multiparty democracy and national sovereignty, can no longer be taken for granted historically; indeed, they have lost their historical foundations. What is NATO without its anticommunism? The growth economy and consumer society with the knowledge of their ecological destructiveness? The welfare state in the global competition of the world economy and in view of the erosion of the old standard labour relationship? Multiparty democracy without its milieu of social and moral consensus? The nation-state in the network of global economic, ecological and security policy dependencies?

Taken together, ambivalence and vacuum mean that the system is not simply hopeless, it is also more open than ever, intellectually and politically.

2

What Comes after Postmodernity? The Conflict of Two Modernities

Sociology is the answer. But what was the question? Is sociology as we practise it, with its theories and controversies, perhaps the answer to the *social issue*? Then is it not time to ask: how can society be an answer to the ecological issue?

Asking it a different way: does the funeral dirge for Marxism, now being publicly celebrated with good justification and bad manners, obscure the obsolescence of the Western sociology of modernization?

In order to interpret the theme of the sociologists' Frankfurt convention, 'the modernization of modern societies', I would like to propose a theoretical distinction that allows us to open up sociology to the challenges of industrial development on the basis of its own conceptual foundations: the distinction between primary and reflexive modernization. Primary modernization means the rationalization of tradition, while reflexive modernization means the rationalization of rationalization.

To date, modernization has always been conceived of, by delimitation from the world of traditions and religions, as a liberation from the constraints of unrestrained nature. What happens if industrial society becomes a 'tradition' to itself? What if its own necessities, functional principles and fundamental concepts are undermined, broken up and demystified with the same ruthlessness as were the supposedly eternal truths of earlier epochs?

The rationalization of rationalization is a key topic in the wake of the end of the East–West conflict and in view of the global challenges of industrial civilization. I would like to pick out three questions to test the viability of this concept:

1 How does the face of industrial society change in reflexive modernization?
2 How can sociology be opened up to the ecological issue?
3 To what extent do primary and reflexive modernization represent
   poles of social conflict in Germany and Europe after the Cold War?

I

What society are we living in? In a society in which everything that was
conceived of as belonging together is being drawn apart: industrial production without industrial society. Industrial society, understood as a
model of the lifeworld in which gender roles, nuclear families and classes
are interlocked, is disappearing, while the engine of industrial dynamism
continues to run, or rather, *because* of the running engine of industrial
dynamism. The same mode of production, the same political system, the
same dynamics of modernization are producing a different society in the
lifeworld: different networks, different circles of relationships, different
lines of conflict and different forms of political alliances for individuals.
How is that possible? Key concepts and variables of industrial society,
class, nuclear family and occupation, were fragmented and shuffled
into new patterns by the expansion of the welfare state following the
Second World War, by the expansion of education, by increasing real
wages and by social and geographical mobility, as well as by increases
in women's work outside the home, in divorce rates and in the flexibility
of paid labour. This perspective contains three theses.

First, industrial society as a *systematic context*, that is, the dynamism of
business, politics and science, is dissolving industrial society as a *context
of experience*. People are being freed from the certainties and standardized
roles of industrial society. Men are no longer automatically fathers, fathers
no longer the sole wage-earners, and sole wage-earners often no longer
husbands. In earlier generations social stratum, income, profession, spouse
and political attitude were generally a unified whole; today this biographical package is disintegrating into its components. For instance, income
is no longer an automatic indicator of place and type of residence, marital
status, political behaviour and so on.

Second, modern society is splitting *into*, on the one hand, the *inside*
of the institutions that preserve the old certainties and normalcies of
industrial society, and, on the other, a variety of lifeworld realities that
are moving further and further from those images. To paraphrase Brecht,
political parties and labour unions may soon find themselves forced to
discharge their voters and members, who are no longer willing to con-
form to the institutionalized image of themselves.

Third, a double problematic results. More and more people are slipping through the normalized gaps in the social safety network (for example, poverty is made inevitable by working conditions so uncertain that wages fall below the eligibility threshold for social insurance). In addition, the institutions of the lifeworld and the consensus through which they once maintained their existence no longer apply (consider the rise of swing voters and opinion poll democracy). This amounts to something I like to call the 'individualization of institutions', for it is no longer possible to conceive of institutions independent of individuals. Conflicts *over* institutional policy break out *within* the institutions.

Industrial production without industrial society: even in its preliminary form, this developmental variant is slippery. Any variation, even any independent variation, of industrial society as a systematic *and* an experiential context is analytically closed off in sociological theory. Marx conceived of industrial society *as* a class society. Capitalism *without* classes is not just a betrayal, it is tantamount to trying to jump out of the window and fly upwards. Talcott Parsons, on the other hand, categorized capitalism as a nuclear family society. The dissolution of gender hierarchies violates the *good manners* of functional prerequisites.

'Adieu to class society' sounds to many as if class society has been overcome. Since no one can seriously claim that, however, in view of the continued existence of social hierarchy, we remain unable to understand the developmental variant that is being considered here, that is, an alteration of the social structure of social inequality that can easily accompany an increase in social inequality, as the increasing gap in incomes in Germany over the past few years attests.

'Adieu' also suggests dissolution. Where the nuclear family is concerned, all joking stops. People get caught in religious and political taboos, and, not least important, in defending their own private world structures.

My intention is not to cover up the balancing necessary here, but only to point out the awkward beginning. Since variation in the basic pattern of the lifeworld is politically and sociologically disallowed, alternative typologies for sociostructural organization in the lifeworld are in practice either non-existent or rudimentary. Beyond the industrial world structures of class, stratum and nuclear family, there is only a loose collection of individuals rustling in the wind.

Let me give a comparison. The theory of industrial society posits various production sectors, and so it is possible to thoroughly explore, work out and discuss the effects of a change of priorities from an industrial to a service society. But, in the case of social structures, there are no anthropological, moral or political alternatives. As long as this is so, even empirical research is stuck in its well-worn groove. The abundant doubts, ambiguities and deviations, the entire fog of the social structure, show up in masses of data that are repeatedly poured into the old categorical bottles. But the diagnosis of continuity when there is no theoretical alternative is empty, not falsifiable.

Consider, for example, research about the nuclear family. There have been radical changes in family structure: cohabitation, informal marriages, exponential increases in the number of single-person households, single parents. Yet, with a few important exceptions, family sociology, especially in Germany, has been busy for years signalling 'all clear'. In the heart of the nuclear family, everything is apparently completely healthy!

We're forced to ask whether German family sociology is wedded to the nuclear family. What must happen for empirical sociology to even consider the possibility of a conceptual reform of its research field? I am certain that even when 70 per cent of the households in large cities are single-person households, a point that is not very far away, our intrepid family sociologists will have millions of bits of data to prove that those 70 per cent are only living alone because they used to live in nuclear families or that they will do so again some day. And if you ask me (I know you cannot, so I will ask myself) why the nuclear family is so stable in Germany, then I will give you my secret answer: because family sociology is so faithful about inquiring into it! Because there is no typology, either in social statistics or sociologically, whose core is not the nuclear family.

One can imagine-and-discuss at least the following alternatives to the traditional nuclear family:

- The entire familial structure is underdifferentiated: that is, not one family, but families.
- Primary relationships fluctuate, along a variety of paths, between the nuclear family and other ways of life.
- Parenthood is divisible; therefore divorce multiplies parenthood, so that physical and social parenthood diverge; children have many parents; kinship networks become multiple and ambivalent.
- High remarriage rates testify to the continuing attractiveness of the nuclear family, but they are only as high as they are because of the frequency of divorce, and high remarriage rates maximize the number of parents and grandparents. New postfamilial, autofamilial and exofamilial networks emerge; behind the facade of the momentary and superficial nuclear family, each individual family member is a member of many families.[1]

The suspicion that the continuity of the nuclear family has its real basis in the continuity of nuclear family *research* is corroborated by parallels from research into German social structure. The alternative to classes was strata. Strata, like classes, are large groups, conceived in terms that are politically paler and less significant. They offer, however, the same metaphor of a social structure as a *torte*, only with more layers and more frosting. Here too, the constancy of the typologies and conceptual schemata is taken to mean that the data are constant, and all of them together are taken to mean that the social structure is constant. And unless we just ignore this type of sociology, we will still be living in this society of nuclear family, class, professions and industry three hundred years from now.

It is also possible, however, to turn the tables on the structural traditionalists. In an empirical stalemate the better theory will dominate. On a closer look, we see that what is being extended into all eternity under the name 'modern society' is actually a hybrid between feudal and industrial society. Homemaking, for instance, as I have learned from women's studies, supports paid labour; it is its backrest and supporting rear leg, so to speak. Both forms of labour arose in complementary fashion and with opposing principles, in the phase of primary industrialization. Homemaking means not having any money of one's own, but also not having any pressure to meet a quota; instead one has people, large and small, screaming for attention around the clock. Certainly it is an indispensable labour, which adheres to women through birth, specifically for having been born female, and through love, or, more precisely, through marriage; it is as permanent as it is unpaid and uninsured. Such a thing can hardly be stable in a milieu of increasing options and market-based individualization. Thus threads of industrial countermodernity extend through the tissue of the old industrial society: let us have universalism, of course, but only up to national and gender boundaries please; let us have freedom to decide and democracy, certainly, but not, please, in key questions of technology and science.

The collapse of Stalinism has again drawn attention to the fact that a social system's claim to be an independent agent depends on one central condition: the consent of individuals to its autonomy. I say 'again' because Hannah Arendt had already made it clear, on the basis of a bitter real-life example, that bureaucracies only become machines through the conscious, or sometimes semi-conscious, culturally mediated efforts of people. Her example was an international intercultural comparison of the bureaucratic organization of the annihilation of the Jews in all its individual steps, rounding up, separating, deporting and so forth. She showed that the bureaucratic machinery that operated so perfectly in Germany was sabotaged in Italy by a traditional aversion to bureaucracy, and was spectacularly sabotaged in Denmark, where members of the royal family and many citizens chose to wear the Star of David.

It was slowed in Bulgaria by spontaneous demonstrations of sympathy from the population, while in Romania it ran almost more smoothly than in Germany.[2] Postwar German sociology has never acknowledged this lesson.

The autonomy of social systems is culturally borrowed. It was possible to forget this so long as the basic forms of the society of individuals and institutional society still corresponded. Once the two societies diverge, the last grand, central illusion of sociology decays: the metaphysics of social systems. Class, nuclear family, marriage, profession, female role, male role, the forms and formulas of consensus, all crumble. The social moulds that political parties and organizations use to build their programmes and their work become indistinct. The systems of social protection, administration of work or family policy preserve an industrial society normalcy that no longer applies for larger and larger groups in the population. All of this means that institutions become individual-dependent, not because the individuals have become powerful but because the institutions have become historically contradictory.

Sociology has so far situated the conflicts outside or on the edges of institutions, in the overlap between 'system and lifeworld' (Habermas). In reflexive modernization, conflicts erupt *inside* the institutions over foundations and developmental alternatives. This applies to women's policy, transportation policy, municipal policy, corporate labour and employment policy, and technology policy, among others. The cultural basis that allows a system to be autonomous is a relic of pre-democratic and, in that sense, premodern ways of life. The stimulation of democracy brings that confusion and quarrelling that is testified to by such diverse phenomena as individual-centred management strategies, concern for business ethics, self-critical lawyers and doctors, feminist professional organizations and many others.

Reflexive modernization deprives commonalities, from the tribal organization to social systems, of their bases. As a thought experiment, it was possible to predict what is now becoming a problem for thought and policy-making. Modernization is a dissolution process; its result is that social standards, from tradition to the categorical imperative, only receive lip service. This does not mean the end of all community, as cultural criticism has been lamenting for over a century now, but the end of all prescribed, retrievable and predictable community, and the beginning of a new type. This new type of community no longer rules from the top down, nor can it be poured into people through the funnel of the functionalist model of socialization. Instead, it must be waited for, won, fought out, invented and negotiated from below. The question arises in response, How is society possible as a social movement of individuals?

II

What does the ecological question mean in this connection? Might it not be wiser for a sociologist to keep silent on this or that question? Where is the guarantee that the ecology issue itself will not dissolve into oblivion at the next turn of the zeitgeist, so that we late converts to ecology would be conducting research without a research subject, or worse, without research funding? Where is the hard core of the ecological issue? What forces or justifies sociological competence beyond moral support and appeals, which are of course open to everyone.

Industrial society is an industrial *production* society. In its development it produces an industrial *consequence* society, its oversized and negative mirror image in everything: pattern, autodynamism, interest, valency, conflict logic, and hysteria. Before, there were prosperity, property, business, the nation-state, social protection. Now there are only unappetizing and unpleasant things that no one wants, things that encounter denial and defensiveness and that must be classified by what they gnaw at: health, life, property, markets, confidence; things that have local dimensions, but that also have international ones, ignoring all the class and system borders of industrial society. Here, too, there is inequality; poverty attracts risks. But the inequalities diminish in the global surplus of risks. Pollutants do not spare the drinking water of directors general.

One could say that this is all nebulous, that it sounds like late Shakespeare. But struggles over how to dispose of things dominate transportation policy, and the question of the location of waste incinerators is not only reaching into chemical and biotechnical laboratories but also affecting food policy, water policy, air policy and agriculture policy. These struggles cause world markets to collapse, threaten entire industries and recreation areas, and create in the population an unstable mood between cynicism and hysteria. In other words: the universal shadow of modernity, the world society of consequences, thwarts the old industrial order. Today, a sociology that looks the other way is a sociology of the past; it no longer understands the society it investigates.

I would like to lay out this assessment in three theses.

First, the model of industrial society conceives of things as being together that are now breaking apart and developing in contrary ways: industrial production society and industrial consequence society. This presumes a distinction between controllable consequences, *risks*, and uncontrollable consequences, *threats*, in industrialism. The criteria for the distinction can be derived from the institutionalized regulatory system itself. The standards that 'rationally' control side-effects have become largely ineffectual. In the chemical and atomic age, all the fundamental concepts of risk management in business, law and politics, including the concepts of accident, insurance protection, the polluter-pays principle, liability and the like, fail in the face of consequences and devastation that can no longer be limited spatially, temporally and/or socially, as could early industrial operating and occupational accidents; nor can they be appropriately calculated and compensated for. Technically, the probability of occurrence may be minimized by the appropriate arrangements, but what threatens us spans generations and nations. We know that the casualties of Chernobyl have not even all been born yet. In the face of consequences of such dimensions, the concepts of accident and the calculation of and compensation for industrial consequences and devastation all fail.

Is there an operational criterion, then, for distinguishing between risks and threats? Very definitely: the denial of private insurance protection. And this applies to the whole spectrum of modern megatechnology.

The environmental problem is by no means a problem of the world surrounding us. It is a crisis of industrial society itself, deeply rooted in the foundations of its institutions and with considerable political resonance. Threats are produced industrially, externalized economically, individualized juridically, legitimized scientifically and minimized politically. This becomes palpable in the fact that (in the best case!) everyone observes the rules, with the result that the oceans, species and forests are dying.

The key to combating destruction of the environment is not found in the environment itself, nor in a different individual morality or in different research or business ethics; by nature it lies in the regulatory systems of the institutions that are becoming historically questionable. Without sociology, the ecological issue will remain opaque to society and impervious to action. A sociology, however, that transfers its experiences of the mutability of society which it has gained from the welfare state to the ecological issue can do more than simply critique ideology to oppose the politically dangerous confusion of nature and society that is now spreading everywhere. Asserting that the central problem of accountability is not amenable to human intervention is simply bad sociology from the craftsman's point of view. Because the question of causality *never* provides an answer to the problem of accountability, the welfare issue could and still can only be grasped in conventions and social agreements. The problem of accountability is an issue of accountability *customs* and accountability *agreements*, hence requiring social models that must be accepted or invented, fought for and pushed through despite resistance.

The welfare state is the first result of these experiences. Sociology can bring this experience to light again with research on the ecological crisis and argue it out in public.

My second thesis is that the industrial production society manufactures its opposite, the global society of industrial consequences, not only in the industrial/technical sense, but also in the social/sociological sense, which amounts to blanket approbation by avoiding the essential problems. Consider the example of acceptability levels.

Acceptability levels both forbid and permit. They permit whatever they do not address. Whatever is permitted is non-toxic, even if it results in permanent poisoning. Acceptability levels thus force a distinction between the permissible, which is officially detoxified (but only officially), and the toxic, which collects in oceans and abdomens. From this one can formulate the law of the social production of threats and devastation: the less is forbidden, the more is officially non-toxic, which poses invisible and uncontrollable long-term threats. The key point is that the official verdict of non-toxicity negates the toxicity of the toxin and, thus, becomes a safe-conduct for pollution.

What Max Weber was not yet able to see, but which must concern us, is the law of modernity, changed in the course of its establishment, according to which the uncontrollability of the consequences grows with the claims to control instrumental rationality. The ecological issue is a special case of this, in which control and non-control, the non-existence of threats and therefore their reproduction and strengthening, coincide and cooperate. We need to reconstruct the instrumental rationality theory of bureaucracy as a Potemkin theory. The administration of uncontrollable things must lead to ridiculous bureaucratic travesties. A wonderful example, fit for a collector, is the idyll of emergency management in the atomic age. Foreign nuclear reactor accidents are not counted, for administrative reasons, while domestic ones are considerate enough to limit their threats to a 29-mile radius, around the nuclear power plant. In this sense, we need to distinguish between the administration of nonsense and the administration of nonsense by nonsensical means.

My third thesis is that repressing and denying threats is a unique type of social activity. The primary industrial conflict, labour versus capital, is overlapped by a negative-sum game of collective self-damaging. Here the disputed advantages are largely exhausted in defining, warding off and accounting for negative consequences. This war game develops its own logic, scenarios, drives, forms of conflict and typical patterns. For instance, it is necessary to defend the arrangements of manufactured unaccountability in the law, in science and in local politics. There are times and cases where it is worthwhile to be obstructionist, and others where dramatizing others' threats whitewashes the risks of one's own products. Playing up the hole in the ozone layer, for instance, favours nuclear energy indirectly and without any biased activity on one's own part, and thus it may occasionally be appropriate to promote the protests of environmental activists whom one would otherwise oppose in the harshest terms.

Once a threat, forest destruction for instance, has been socially recognized as such, one must at least change one's language and place one's own products and productions in the service of this great new cause. Even more, there is a rush to exploit the threat. Its causal architecture opens future markets and lays pipelines for research funding. Certainly, everything is unaccountable, multifunctional and cross-linked beyond causality. But now this is suddenly no longer the case. Now it is time for symbolic action, and there the old monocausality prevails. In the end, the causes – of forest destruction for instance – are not trucks, not the lack of a speed limit, not coal-fired power plants; rather, following the old industrial society formula, the lack of a catalytic converter becomes the lightning rod for citizen protest. The selection of the scapegoat cannot be made and justified based on scientific data and arguments alone. Therefore it is handed to the sociology of social design on a silver platter.

The key point, however, goes far beyond this. Ecological conflict logic is not played out by different agents or different institutions in different arenas but, rather, by the same industrial society agents (supplemented by social movements and citizens' groups). The prevailing system of rules of the game is shuffled together with another one. People play Parcheesi and blindman's bluff at the same time.

Labour unions, for instance, can find themselves involuntarily pushed over to management's side by attacks from ecological groups. Not only does their position in the next round of collective bargaining suffer from this, but also the white-collar staff that they are wooing may decide to join the management directly. The throttling of local transportation policy inflames the factional struggles within the traditional labour party, which means that the profile of the party begins to blur together with that of their conservative opponent or the greens. Since this issue can only be constructed or destroyed within their frame of reference, scientists find themselves in the both pleasant and embarrassing position of serving all masters: they direct the denial, determination and removal of the threats. In general terms, the institutions' objectives become ambiguous and shady, not infrequently enriched by the other side's objective; and thus not only do their profiles and structures blur, they also become dependent on actions and individuals.

The ecological crisis is depriving institutions of the basis of their auto-nomy. Delegating contradictions means that one can distinguish justice from injustice and rules from pronouncements. Everything must be re-interpreted. The ecological crisis is a liberating process within and against bureaucracy. The rigidity of roles that functionalism asserts collapses in the shifting of stage sets and conflict scenarios. In one sense, the ecolo-gical crisis can be compared to the sixteenth-century Peasant Revolts: the players are released from functional ties, just as the peasants were released from their ties to the liege-lord. This is not an abrupt but a creeping process. Prosperity and the production of threats yield a defen-sive performance of what is still considered necessary rather than consent – while simultaneously constructing escape tunnels. I nearly said, as in Stalinism.

The two parts of my diagnosis fit together. In reflexive modernization, the institutions of industrial society lose their historical foundations and become contradictory, conflicted and dependent on the individual; they prove to be in need of consent and of interpretation and open to internal coalitions and social movements. The question of the individual is raised once again, not directly but via the detour of institutional criti-cism. This all remains politically ambiguous, however. For instance, reflex-ive modernization serves not only the ecological opposition but also the opposition to that opposition. What results from it and what can be made of it remain open, and must remain open, if the theory is not to come into conflict with itself.

The theory of reflexive modernization calls the diagnostic bite of competing theories into question. It differs from crisis theories, claiming that the pressing questions are the expression of triumphs, not crises, of industrialism. In contradiction to functionalism, it asserts the self-denormalization of industrial society. In contradiction to theories of post-modernity, it insists that modernity is just beginning. And, in opposition to theories of social and ecological limits, it points to the transformation of the premises and the coordinate system of industrial modernity.

III

We postwar Germans believe unwaveringly in the compatibility of an economic boom and private political conservatism in some form or another. This very potent utopia is a kind of yodelling high-tech that attempts to fuse the day before yesterday with the day after tomorrow, perfectly and forever. If my diagnosis is correct, the modernization of modern societies, with its unleashed dynamism, is smashing this petty-bourgeois supermodernism to bits. Modernity is not a hansom cab one can get out of on the next corner if one no longer likes it, as Max Weber said, and this still applies when modernity turns the corner into reflexive application.

It is also true, however, that the rush to adopt the Western model in post-Stalinist Eastern Europe and the integration of East Germany with West Germany represent a revival of primary modernization in Germany and Europe, with hopes for the economic growth of that earlier stage; but also with the return of its nationalism and ethnic rivalries. The truth lies in conceiving of both alternatives together. The Germany that is coming into being is a Germany with *two* modernities, and it must work out a European, indeed a global, conflict within itself.

The contrasts between primary and reflexive modernization are also opening to discussion a fundamental political conflict. In all aspects of social development, the praxis of 'more of the same', which drew new strength from the collapse of the Stalinist bloc, is encountering doubters and people trying to restrain its effects, people who are searching for ways to an alternative modernity.

This is becoming a personal, everyday conflict as well as a fundamental, political one, and it is occurring on all levels: neighbourhood, municipality, nation, world, with diffuse and fluctuating alliances and with no recognizable principles for compromise. The ability to tolerate, to endure insoluble contradictions and to view the world from an opposing viewpoint has never been so urgent and, at the same time, so endangered as it is in the impending conflict of the two modernities, in which people must learn how to laugh at themselves. What is needed is self-limitation, that is, settling for imperfection.

In casting off Stalinism, 'freedom', the magic word of European modernity, has taken on a new, even a German bourgeois, sound. But the Western industrial countries are not free either. They are freer. Their claim to freedom and democracy conceals the industrial compulsion they embrace.

It has always been the same. The ancient Greeks drew the line at the slaves in their demands for equality. And slavery lasted for thousands of years: Thoreau, the master dreamer of the American Dream, was still struggling against slavery, which was defended at the time as being economically indispensable (not unlike the justifications for nuclear energy and economic expansion today). The limit for science was religion. 'Human equality' was always 'male equality'. Just a historical moment ago, an eternal law prevailed: democracy ends at the wall of the East–West conflict. And today, limits still prevail: self-determination and democracy, why of course, but not if it conflicts with the imperialism of technology, science and industry.

This is central: there is no difference in principle between considering slave labour to be immutable, recognizing equality only for males and declaring the absolute dominance of technology and the fatalistic transfiguration of ecological self-destruction.

The conflict of the future will no longer be between East and West, between communism and capitalism, but between the countries, regions and groups on the way to primary modernity and those that are attempting to relativize and reform this project self-critically, based on their experience of modernity. The conflict of the future will be the conflict of two modernities, which will battle over the compatibility of survival and human rights for all citizens of the earth. Making this conflict understandable could become an essential task for sociology.

3

The Withering Away of Solidarity: Places without Community and Communities without Places

From across the Atlantic one hears the communitarians' call for *new values*. There is no doubt the country needs that, but wherever one looks, there are references to 'individualization' (which should not be confused with 'Thatcherism', see below). If this continues, then at least the use of the word should soon be threatened with punishment.

This is something ancient, or at least a basic phenomenon of modernity. Max Weber worked out how the individual is gradually removed from the certainty of religious salvation and discharged into the unresolvable values and world-view conflicts of society as it becomes disenchanted. Karl Marx speaks ironically of the wage labourer's 'double freedom'. He is freed from traditional ties to the soil and free to be exploited on the labour market. Georg Simmel reconstructed how financial relationships break up local, encrusted social groups and link together global networks on an abstract level.

But for all the similarities to these themes brought up in the late nineteenth century, people today are not being 'discharged' from feudal-religious certainties *into* the world of industrial society, but *from* the security of industrial society into the turbulence of global risk society. Not least important of all, their lives are being burdened with the most varied and contradictory global and personal risks.

Industrial society thus presumes resources of nature and culture, whose existence it builds upon, but whose substance is gradually used up in the course of modernization as it becomes established. This also applies to cultural ways of life (nuclear family and gender order, for instance) and to social labour assets (housewives' labour, for instance, which was not recognized as labour, but none the less was what actually made the husbands' paid labour possible in the first place).

The collective or group-specific reservoirs of meaning (faith or class consciousness, for example) in traditional culture (which also supported Western democracies and business societies until well into the twentieth century with their lifestyles and notions of security) are being drained and this has the effect that all the work of making definitions is asked of individuals.

Opportunities, dangers and ambivalences of biography that might previously have been mastered in the family group or the London street villages, by recourse to status rules or social classes, must now be perceived, interpreted and worked out by individuals themselves. The opportunities and burdens of defining and mastering the situation thus shift to individuals, even though they may be incapable of making the inevitable decisions soundly and responsibly in the light of the interests, morality and consequences at stake, because of the high complexity of the social context.

Disembedding and re-embedding

'Individualization' does *not* mean a lot of the things that many people wish it meant in order to be able to refute it more easily. It does not mean market individualism or Thatcherism, atomization, isolation, the lack of any relationships for a free-floating individual, nor does it mean (as is sometimes alleged) individuation, emancipation or autonomy: the revival of the defunct bourgeois individual.

Instead, it means, first, the *dis*embedding of the ways of life of industrial society (class, stratum, gender role, family), and second, the *re*-embedding of new ones, in which individuals must produce, stage and cobble together their biographies themselves. The standard biography becomes a chosen or reflexive biography, a 'do-it-yourself biography' (Ronald Hitzler).[1]

This applies not only to the typical class or woman's biography but also to the bureaucratically prescribed standard biography in real existing non-socialism. This is now disintegrating, after the fall into modernity, into a heap of difficult-to-decide decisions. The halving of the birth, marriage and divorce rates in the former East Germany within one (!) year attest dramatically to this.

Individualization is thus by no means based on a free decision. People are damned to individualization, using Sartre's terms. This involves a compulsion, paradoxical of course, to produce, arrange and stage, not just their own biographies, but also their moral, social and political commitments, under the conditions of the welfare state, such as education, the labour market, labour and social welfare legislation and so on. Where everything has been transformed into decisions that are becoming risky, even traditional marriage will have to be chosen as a personal risk from now on and justified and lived out with all its built-in contradictions.

Previously, status-based marriage prohibitions and rules dominated, while today it is the anonymous requirements of wage labour and social protections, but with an essential difference. While the narrow traditional patterns forced the individuals into togetherness, the norms today force people to build up and lead a life *of their own*, on pain of economic disadvantage.

Women too must go through an educational and professional career of their own inside and beneath marriage and motherhood, if they do not wish to face ruin in case of divorce or be supported as 'lifelong unemployed people'. Marriage and family thus become a juggling act with diverging biographies, with no patent remedy to insure cohesion.

Collective fate

The welfare state, whose benefits presume participation in the labour market, is an experimental arrangement for the conditioning of ego-centric ways of life. One may prescribe a general 'inoculation of duty' against this, but it will be of no help as long as circumstances ordain the opposite. Anyone who wishes to restore the good old solidarity must turn back the wheel of modernization, that is to say, push women out of the labour market, not just covertly, through maternity payments and measures to make housework more attractive, but openly, and not only out of the labour market, but out of education as well. The wage differential between men and women would have to be increased and ultimately equality before the law would have to be rescinded. It would be necessary to check whether the evil had not perhaps started with universal suffrage. Accordingly, family policy can easily degenerate into the attempt to chase women out of the labour market – and get one's shirts ironed in the process.

Individualization therefore, to pick out one peculiarity, is a collective fate, not an individual one. This does not mean that individualization is only experienced and suffered passively. No one wants to go backwards. The sacrifice of a bit of hard-won freedom is something that everyone, man or woman, expects only of others.

But what drives millions of people in all the countries of the globe, seemingly as individuals but actually following a generally shared dream, to break out of marriage and live together 'in sin' outside of the comfortable legal safety net? Is that a type of 'ego fever' that can be treated by hot compresses of 'us'? Not likely.

A new relationship between individual and society is announcing itself here. Communal spirit can no longer be ordained from the top down, but must instead be freed up by questioning and brought about in struggling through individual and biographical problems. It must be agreed on, negotiated, justified and experienced; it must become aware of and prove itself against the centrifugal force of biographies. That this need not end up as entrapment in a retreat into private life is something shown by the emergence of citizens' initiatives, which have at least been able to put their concerns, (environment, women, right-wing violence) on the political agenda against the will of the parties.

Trapdoors into poverty

But aren't these fair-weather pictures of a society in a prosperous niche that seem oddly dated given the storms that have beset us – war in Europe and over 3.5 million *registered* unemployed people in Germany? In the former West Germany we really did experience a type of 'comprehensively insured individualization' (high prosperity, high social security) that is now beset by the turbulences of distribution of the shortage. Individualization has never meant the dissolution of social inequality, but so far always its *intensification*.

First of all, the income gap is widening. Second, more and more groups are afflicted, at least temporarily, by poverty and unemployment. Third, these tend less and less to follow social stereotypes and are therefore harder and harder to identify and thus organize as a political force. Not just unemployment, but divorce as well, are trapdoors into poverty; many women are 'only a husband away' from poverty (and vice versa). Fourth, under the conditions of individualization, people must increasingly cope with as an individual failure that which was previously treated communally as a class fate. Statistical fates of millions of people are turning into personal guilt, conflicts and neuroses.

All of this means that *social* crises increasingly appear to be *individual* ones and tend less and less to be perceived as social and treated politically. Hence the likelihood grows of a broad variety of irrational outbreaks of all types, not least in the form of violence against everything labelled 'foreign'. Precisely in individualized society, lines of conflict arise along socially identifiable features: race, skin colour, gender, ethnic identity, age, homosexuality or physical disability.

Will we be successful in linking up with the demands and promises of the individualization process now underway and regrouping the individuals beyond class and status as self-confident subjects of their own personal, political and social concerns? Or will the last bastions of social and political praxis be melted away in the continuing individualization as society skids from an annoyance with parties to an annoyance with the state itself, which will leave nothing out of the question, not even, in new and insidious forms, a modernization of barbarism?

Subpolitics: the individuals return

There is a local bias in the diagnosis of disintegrating (reflexive) modernity. The assumption is that community and political engagement are bound to a specific place. But the relationship between community and locality has been transformed. Globalization of political engagement means there are localities without communities and transnational (political) 'communities' which are not related to a specific location (see Albrow 1996b). The socially most astonishing and surprising, yet perhaps the least understood, phenomenon of the 1980s is the unexpected renaissance of a *global political subjectivity*, outside and inside the institutions. In this sense, it is no exaggeration to say that social movements, citizen initiative groups and non-governmental organizations have taken power politically. They were the ones who put the issue of an endangered world on the agenda, against the resistance of the established parties. Nowhere is this so clear as in the spectre of the new 'lip service morality' that is haunting Europe. The compulsion to engage in the ecological salvation and renewal of the world has by now become universal. It unites the conservatives with the socialists, and the chemical industry with its green arch-critics.

One almost has to fear that the chemical industry will follow up on its full-page ads and re-establish itself as a conservation association. Admittedly, this is all just packaging, programmatic opportunism, and now and then perhaps really intentional rethinking. The actions and the points of origin of the facts remain largely untouched. Yet it remains true: the themes of the future, which are now on everyone's lips, did not originate from the farsightedness of the rulers or from the struggle in parliament – and certainly not from the cathedrals of power in business, science and the state.

The systems are bankrupt

'The politicians are insulted that people are less and less interested in them,' writes Hans Magnus Enzensberger, 'but they ought to ask themselves what is the cause of this? I suspect that the politicians have fallen victim to a self-deception, that they have an incorrect definition of politics . . . The core of today's politics is the capacity for self-organization' (1991: 230f.). Self-organization does not mean the liberal topos of the free play of social forces, but rather subpolitics, the shaping of society from the bottom up. The site and subject of the definition of the common good, of the guarantee of public peace and historical recollection are to be found less inside and more outside of the political system.

This applies not just to the western, but also to the eastern part of Europe. There the citizens' groups started from zero with no organization, in a system of surveilled conformity, and yet, lacking even copying machines or telephones, they were able to force the ruling group to retreat and collapse just by assembling on the streets. This rebellion of real existing individuals against a 'system' that allegedly dominated them all the way into the capillaries of day-to-day existence is inexplicable and inconceivable within the prevailing categories and theories. But it is not only the planned economy which is bankrupt. Systems theory, which conceives of society as independent of the subject, has been just as thoroughly refuted. In a society without consensus, devoid of a legitimating core, it is evident that even a single gust of wind, caused by the cry for freedom, can bring down the whole house of cards of power.

Of course one could say, 'water under the bridge'. The insight might be difficult for many people, but even the extreme right-wing headhunters who have been mobilizing in the streets of Germany since the summer of 1992 against 'foreigners' (and whomever they consider to be such), as well as the covert and unnerving support they find all the way to the top of politics – yes even this mob – is using and acting out the opportunities of subpolitics. It can always be seized and used by the opposite side or party for the opposite goals. What appeared to be a 'loss of consensus', an 'unpolitical retreat to private life', 'new inwardness' or 'caring for emotional wounds' in the old understanding of politics, can, when seen from the other side, represent the struggle for a new dimension of politics.

Just about everything, it would seem, argues against this rebirth of politics. The issues that are disputed in the established political arenas, or one would be tempted to say, for which antagonisms are simulated there, scarcely have any explosive power left that could yield sparks of politics. Accordingly, it is becoming less and less possible all the time to derive decisions from the partisan programmatic superstructure.

Conversely, the organizations of the parties, the trade unions and so forth make use of the freely available masses of issues to hammer together the programmatic prerequisites for their continued existence. Internally and externally, so it seems, politics is losing both its polarizing and its creative, utopian quality.

That diagnosis rests, in my view, on a category error, the equation of politics and state, politics and the political system, and the correction of that error does not completely deprive the diagnosis of its elements of truth, but it does not validate it either. People expect to find politics in the arenas prescribed for it, and they expect politics to be performed by the duly authorized agents: parliament, political parties, trade unions and so on. If the clocks of politics stop there, then it seems that politics as a whole has stopped ticking. That overlooks the fact that an immobility of the governmental apparatus and its subsidiary agencies may very well accompany the mobility of the agents on all possible levels of society, that is to say, politics may peter out as subpolitics is activated.

Fragile coalitions

Let me cite one example: the increase of welfare and the increase of hazards mutually condition one another. To the extent that people become (publicly) aware of this, the defenders of safety are no longer sitting in the same boat with the planners and producers of economic wealth. The coalition of technology and business becomes shaky, because technology can increase productivity, but at the same time it puts legitimacy at risk. The judicial order no longer fosters social peace, because it sanctions and legitimates disadvantages along with the threats, and so on.

The annoyance with parties that is now so popular is also a form of civil self-denial. It is blind to and blinds others to the capabilities of subpolitics. People look for politics in the wrong place, with the wrong terms, on the wrong floors of offices and on the wrong pages of the newspapers. Those decision-making areas which had been protected by politics in conventional industrial capitalism – the private sector, business, science, municipalities, everyday life and so on – are caught in the storms of political conflicts. An important point here is that how far this process goes, what it means and where it leads are in turn dependent on political decisions, which cannot simply be taken, but must be formed, programmatically filled out and transformed into possibilities for action. Subpolitics determines politics, opening it up and empowering it. These possibilities of an invention of politics after the Cold War are what we must unfold and illuminate.[2]

4

Perspectives on a Cultural Evolution of Work

I

If involvement with the future of society is enjoying a boom today, then this is the surest symptom that something has begun to break up: the belief in progress which until now has stabilized the future. So long as people answer the annoying question, 'what do we do now?', which comes up for every new generation, on the pattern of the concept of progress, that is, 'let us improve, expand, enlarge and multiply what we have' (two cars per family instead of one, etc.), an involvement with the social future is possible and superfluous in equal measure. It is possible because the future is conceived of in continuity with the past and the present, and it is more or less irrelevant for the same reason.

Like many other things, the future becomes a topic of interest only where it becomes problematic. Wrestling with issues of the future in this sense is a measure of how the past is losing its power to determine the present. It is being replaced by the future, hence something non-existent, constructed, even fictitious as the 'cause' of current experience and action. We become active today in order to prevent, ameliorate or preclude the problems and crises of tomorrow or the day after tomorrow, or perhaps we opt not to do so. Threats to the future influence current planning and decision-making and impair the general well-being and the conditions of life for people today. Bottlenecks 'predicted' in models of the labour market reflect directly back on educational behaviour; anticipated or impending unemployment is an essential determinant of current conditions of life and attitudes towards it; the predicted devastation of the environment and the nuclear threat are upsetting an entire society and have been able to motivate large portions of the younger generation to protest. No particular preference for paradoxical statements is required to draw this all together into the *thesis* that in the conflict with the future we are involved with a *'projected variable', a 'projected cause' of current (personal and political) action, whose relevance and significance increases in direct proportion to its unpredictability* and which we invent and (are compelled to) design in order to define and organize our current activity.[1]

Threats to the future, its tendency to become open and uncertain, are an essential measure of the instability, but also the historicality of a society, of its affliction with crises, but also its political character, and of the conflicts over values and objectives that open up in that society, as well as the compulsions and opportunities to act in it. Present-day society becomes dependent on something that can neither be perceived nor explained (in causal terms) because it simply does not exist and can therefore never shake off its fictitious character. Nevertheless, it is intensely pertinent and is even, one could say, experienced physically (anxiety!); it is able to activate action today to an extent that scientific statements about the present and the past seldom achieve. To the extent that the future becomes open, endangered and uncertain, it becomes a novel and central 'theatre of battle' for calling into question and reshaping present-day society. In this sense, the thesis of the cultural evolution of work which is to be developed in the present chapter means the disappearance of a predictable future and the outbreak and virulence of conflicts over the future in processes of societal labour themselves. This connection between culture and work will be explained and elaborated in three developmental stages (contrasted with one another to emphasize their nature as ideal types).

First, as the background of my argumentation, I would like to show how the concept of progress which prevailed in industrial states into the 1960s can be viewed as an intermeshing of individual, economic and social designs of the future. The framework of the future is thus pre-ordained in the continuity of past and present; under these conditions, the future is not an issue and not a problem.

Second, this only begins to change where such harmonious progress begins to break up, and where the substance, goal and criterion of 'progress' are assessed more and more controversially. Only under these conditions of an emerging lack of consensus on personal and social futures does the significance of the influence of cultural expectations and norms on the arrangement of economic and labour processes stand out. If one wished, one could say that the connection between the Protestant ethic and capitalistic economic activity demonstrated by Max Weber proves its significance once again where it breaks up and thus forces itself to be continued under different premises and with different consequences. Such an interpretation is suggested by developments in the current and the coming century in Western industrial countries.

Third, the cultural evolution of work achieves a real breakthrough only when the emerging threats to the future have taken on a degree of urgency and inevitability that is comparable to the pressure that resulted from the immiseration of broad segments of the working class in the nineteenth century. Only to the extent that the emerging issues of the future turn into threats to present-day existence – as is beginning to appear today in the conflicts over the destruction of the environment, the development and use of nuclear energy and weapons, the criticism of medicine, experts and bureaucracy – do the scope and potential for change in the cultural evolution of labour become fully visible. The concept of and criteria for 'progress' and 'modernity' begin to change themselves and, in the process, the substance, objectives and organizational forms of societal labour.

II

At the beginning of this century, the cultural influence on the system of labour and the economy was the centre of attention for a number of classical studies and authors in social science. Max Weber demonstrated how important Calvinist religious ethics and the 'inner-worldly asceticism' inherent in them were to the origin and establishment of 'professionalism' and capitalistic economic activity. Thorstein Veblen argued more than half a century ago that the laws of economics do not remain effectively unchanged and cannot be understood independently, but are instead completely bound to the value system of society. If social values change, economic principles must also be transformed. If, for example, the majority of the population rejects the values of economic growth (whatever their reason may be), our thinking about the structuring of labour, the criteria for productivity and the direction of economic development becomes dubious, and a new sort of pressure for political action comes into being. In this sense, Weber and Veblen argue (in different ways) that labour and business remain fundamentally tied in multiple ways into the system of cultural values, the prevailing normative expectations and the value orientations of people.[2]

If this clearly evident insight, also asserted by a number of other authors,[3] has scarcely attained any significance beyond lip service in the meantime this ought to be attributed to the fact that, in oversimplified terms, the value system remained essentially *stable* into the 1960s. A 'variable' that is constant goes unseen and is thus not really a 'variable' at all, so that its significance and influence may go unrecognized. This changes abruptly wherever such stability begins to crumble. The significance of the culturally normative background consensus for the structuring and development of industrial labour becomes visible only during its dissolution, posthumously, one could say. It is my thesis that, during postwar development, this normatively cultural stability became concrete in the form of *faith in progress* and in concrete experience of advance. Transcending social and class antagonisms, this industrial consensus on progress was the crucial cultural background constant for the structuring of work and business, a factor whose importance is directly proportional to its self-evidence and lack of recognition. In the postwar recovery, economic, social and individual 'progress' was tangibly intermeshed in (West) Germany (but in other industrial countries as well). 'Economic growth', the 'increase of productivity' and 'technological innovations' were not simply economic objectives that met the self-interest of entrepreneurs in increasing their capital; they led, in a manner visible to everyone, to the reconstruction of society and a 'democratization' of formerly exclusive living standards. This intermeshing of individual, social and economic interests and objectives in the pursuit of 'progress', as understood in economic and scientific-technical terms, succeeded in so far as the boom actually took hold and lasted, that is to say, the pie to be cut up became bigger and bigger and everyone was able to get a share of this growth (even with unchanged relations of inequality).

Under these conditions, the value system of the people, their symbols of success and the criteria for their self-respect and judgements made of them by others were clear, unambiguous, universally comprehensible and related to the criteria of economic success and technological development. In this respect, the predominating interpretation of 'progress' had a clearly middle-class character:

- The economic well-being of the nuclear family symbolized the success of one's own work; the family was considered an 'emotional refuge' in the harsh world of competition and pressure to achieve; it was the real source of enjoyment in life and simultaneously the central space in which 'life was lived'.
- A clear gender-specific division of labour existed inside the family; the male role was that of breadwinner; women found 'happiness' in 'living for others', in their role as wife, mother, cook, housekeeper, etc.
- Consumer goods and their hierarchy were clear indicators of personal success, which was valued as such individually and socially: a single family house (with lawn), a car (differentiated according to price, brand,

petrol consumption, amount of chrome trim, etc.), a refrigerator, washing machine, television set (each in a hierarchy of technical perfection); all these status symbols combine technological progress, economic growth and individual success in exemplary fashion.

- Particular characteristics of these value orientations and cultural expectations were thus their market dependence and market character; the hopes of people and their opportunities for consumption were two sides of the same coin, and their expectations of the future could equally well be expressed in categories of 'market gaps' and technological innovations; furthermore, it was the character of privateness which simultaneously held deviations from traditional norms (in sexuality, in education and so forth) in check.
- Both the market character and the privateness guaranteed the integrative social character of this values system.

What was considered success and what was not were clear and unambiguous, tangible for everyone, so to speak, and thus of great social visibility and obligation. In this way, such completely different parameters as personal and social identity, the expansion of market opportunities and technological progress remained interrelated and intermeshed in a manner that everyone could tangibly experience. The experience of progress (linked, among other things, to the conditions of economic stability, the expansion of education and the expansion of the welfare state) created space for a social obligation which, beyond antagonisms of interest and class, tied together individual interests, economic expansion and the common good in the motto of progress: 'more of the same'.

As a 'cultural background constant', this industrial consensus on progress affects the design of work processes and prescribes possibilities for action which were taken for granted for a long time (for historical reasons).

It is expressed initially in the 'self-evidence' (learned and produced in the wake of industrialization) with which the working population accepts *uniform, general and standardized regulations for the employment of its labour power*: standardized forms of compensation, the uniform norm of full-time work throughout life, standardized processes, contents and results of work, and so on.[4] This 'self-evident willingness', acquired in historical learning processes, to subordinate one's own demands, creative interests and life needs to standardized uniform regulations for the employment of labour power is now diminishing, forcing private and governmental enterprises, but trade unions as well, to rethink things, and raising new types of organizational problems.

The background consensus simultaneously permits a clear determination of the boundaries between the working and the non-working populace. The social reference groups involved in this were specified relatively clearly and were relatively calculable. In essence, the working populace meant the 'husband working full-time throughout his life'; women, in the vast majority of cases, worked outside the home only so long as they absolutely had to do so, that is, so long as there were no children or when it appeared directly necessary to protect the standard of living. But, on the one hand, as mothers also lay claim to paid employment, the boundaries of the working population begin to become more unclear and more unpredictable, because the forms of compensation and the regulation of work times are pluralized and individualized. On the other, the uniform definition of unemployment (with all the social and legal regulations based on it) begins to totter. Isn't a man or woman who is 'only' willing to take on a full-time job temporarily or a part-time job permanently, according to a plan to be negotiated, also unemployed?

In the traditional value system, the expenditure of labour power is tied into the standards of the male gender role stereotype. 'Male' labour power dominates quantitatively and hierarchically; in personality, identity and biography, the man embodies 'professionalism', which can serve as a self-evident basis for the design of work processes. The man's 'success' is essentially connected to economic and professional success; only a secure income makes it possible to satisfy the 'masculine ideal' of the 'good provider' and the 'caring husband and father'. In this respect, the socially approved and lasting satisfaction of sexual needs is tied to economically measurable success. Conversely, this means, of course, that in order to achieve these goals, a man must 'do his best' at work, internalize constraints of a career, and overtax, even 'exploit' himself. This structure of the 'masculine working capacity' is in turn the functional prerequisite for corporate discipline strategies of reward and control. This changes radically when even male success is no longer measured in the criteria of income and career. Where this link between male identity, professional identity and familial identity is loosened or broken, men too can permit other demands and can develop and practise a new attitude towards work.

III

That this 'status and consumption-oriented' value system is crumbling, and with it the consensus on progress, which gathered together individual, social and economic demands, is no longer disputed in ordinary life, the public sphere, science or politics (although there are very different valuations and consequences). There is disagreement over how far this cultural evolution actually extends, what it comprises, which population groups are affected by it, in what way and with what reactions, whether it is a transient or a permanent, possibly even an intensifying phenomenon, to what extent it is tied to boom conditions and will fade away with those conditions, and to what extent the observations so far are appropriate and supported methodologically, and so on.[5]

Transcending these differences and antagonisms, however, the 'decay of bourgeois society', a topic of literature and art since the beginning of this century, has now been confirmed by the results of empirical social research in the form of a deep-seated revolution in the cultural expectations and value ideas of large parts of the populace. It started at the latest in the early 1970s, not only in West Germany, but in all the other Western industrial countries as well. As an interim result of numerous studies and discussions, Helmut Klages summarizes the course of this 'transformation of values' as follows:

> There is a tendency for a lowering of rank particularly for those values which pertain to the obligation for ethically justified obedience to and willingness to follow externally postulated expectations of order and achievement while renouncing opportunities to fulfil one's own drives. One could also say that this involves a reversal of the willingness and ability to be ascetic, as well as the ability and inclination to accept things as they are.
>
> Summarizing once again, one can say that the 'Protestant ethic', which Max Weber was once willing to describe as an 'iron cage' guaranteed by the process of modernization, is fading away. In contrast, all those values which favour the assertion of the needs of self-development and the need for self-referential experiences of fulfilment are elevated in rank, whether these involve acting out one's own competence, living out emotional strivings and needs, or realizing the objectives of the ideal design of the world and society with which one is very personally 'identified'. (1983: 341)

One can argue against these results of public opinion research that they may express changes in the value attitudes and value orientations of people, but not their *behaviour*, which might still be characterized by quiet conformity. This first of all demands a contextualization of the results of values research in terms of culture in the lifeworld. These findings can also be interpreted as consequences of the loss of tradition in class cultures and the break-up of socio-moral milieus in the wake of the economic boom and postwar development of the welfare state in Western democracies. There has been a special surge of *individualization* of life situations and life paths (and the orientations related to them) here (moreover, with constant or possibly even intensifying inequality relations). People are removed by mobility, education, competition, legal regulations, market relationships and so on from traditional commitments to the milieus of their birth and are turned over to their individual 'labour market fate', with all the concomitant risks and opportunities.[6]

In this way, the hopes and orientations of the people begin to detach themselves to some extent from the standardized 'criteria of progress' (career, opportunities for consumption, levels of income, and so on) and yet they remain committed to them in many ways (more on that later). Thus, from the 1960s and 1970s, it has become surprisingly clear that, for a large and growing portion of the population, the goal of personal success no longer coincides with the status symbols of professional success. A variety of conditions and developments no doubt lay behind this: the saturation of households with essential or labour-saving products and technologies, the expansion of education, processes of social and geographical mobility, the legal regulation of labour relations, the reduction of working hours and many others. The loosening of social norms and the transformation of the forms and objectives of relationships in the family, the repercussions of the women's movement on marriage and work within the family, the environmental movement and the accompanying and intensifying fundamental critique of industrialization and science, the possible transformation of progress into risks and threats, as has been seen in disputes over nuclear energy and nuclear weapons: all of these are probably essential in this connection.

It is possible to distinguish two systematic trends that characteristically interpenetrate, supplement and amplify one another in this listing of very heterogeneous developments and influencing factors. In my eyes, these substantiate the profound effect and long-term nature of the cultural evolution that has been set in motion. On the one hand, large groups in the lifeworld such as social classes and strata have a waning importance for how people lead their lives. Something like a collective 'wage-labourer's fate' (protected by the welfare state), even though it is becoming binding on more and more groups in the population, can be perceived and reconstructed only by passing through the 'eye of the needle' of individualized ways of life, destinies and forms of consciousness. In the wake of this individualization, a pluralization of lifestyles and value attitudes across the lines of social classes occurs[7] and is being tested and advanced by a variety of new social movements.

On the other hand, the *follow-on problems and costs* of techno-economic progress were investigated more and more urgently and with greater public effect in the 1960s and 1970s by various groups in the scientific intelligentsia and presented in the sense of a 'crisis of the future' of techno-scientific civilization. While the voices and commentaries of culture critics have followed the triumphal march of industrialization like a shadow from the very beginning, without being able to delay it in any way, in this new phase there is a historically novel *domination of the criticism of civilization and progress by science*. Scientifically illuminating and publicly pillorying damage to health, destruction of nature, environmental pollution, technological risks, self-inflicted nuclear threats and so on, in conjunction with social movements, does more than just unleash a wave of scientifically underpinned critiques of technology and progress (taking practical effects and risks as a starting point). As paradoxical as it sounds, it also opens up new markets and opportunities for expansion for a stagnating economic and technological development.[8] In this manner, two historical trends of the critique of progress interpenetrate one another long-term and through all political changes and 'reversals': the partial independence of people's value orientations from the criteria and categories of techno-economic development in the wake of individualization processes *and* the increasingly scientific nature of the threats to the future provoked by 'progress' itself.

In consequence, the traditional social forms of 'bourgeois society' – class, stratum, wage labour, professions, marriage – are becoming relativized and called into question as forms of a formerly self-evident plan of life and the future. The 'evolution of individualization' taking place in constantly renewed surges (in the Renaissance, for instance or in the nineteenth century) is extended and propelled forward all the way into the family (by women working outside the home and the constraints for education of children, for instance). This strengthens the collective search for a personality of one's own and for less conformist, more self-determined, personally characterized lifestyles, which at the same time continually open up new markets for mass consumption. Regardless of how one explains this development in detail, the search for self-realization is developing its own cultural meanings as it affects more and more groups. Some of these overlap the traditional status criteria of professional success, but many no longer do so. In the limit case and in individual social circles and subcultures, this process may go to the opposite extreme, so that *failure* in profession and career is now evaluated as a sign of personal integrity and the search for identity, while someone who points to his professional success is not only not 'in', but is viewed sceptically and probed in search of a 'deformity of identity'.

Now this development does not include all population groups equally by any means; rather, it is essentially a product of the younger generation, of better education and higher income, while the older, poor and less well-educated portions of the populace clearly continue to be tied to the value system of the 1950s and its status symbols.[9]

The relationship between 'old' and 'new' values, expectations and success symbols is extraordinarily complex. Only a minority unambiguously rejects the consumption-oriented symbols of prestige and success. These are the groups that migrate into the so-called 'informal sector', the niches and cliques of 'alternative culture' – in part due to the pressure of a tight labour market and growing unemployment figures – and try out and implement new styles of communal living and working.[10] In contrast both to the old as well as the broad majority of the new conceptions of values and success, the search for self-fulfilment leads here to a reversal of the principle of progress; 'more of the same' becomes 'less but more varied', less money, fewer possessions, smaller, easier-to-understand institutions and work situations, but development of a variety of personal lifestyles and developmental possibilities. This rejection is not shared, characteristically, by the overwhelming majority of those who are affected by the new value orientations. On the contrary, success, even as measured in conventional categories, is assessed as important, indeed even necessary, but not sufficient.[11] The conventional symbols of success (income, career, status, etc.) no longer fulfil people's deep psychological needs for self-discovery and self-confirmation, their hunger for a 'fulfilled life'. 'In effect, they demand full enjoyment as well as full employment' (D. Yankelovich 1979: 11).

In the 1950s and 1960s, people responded clearly and unambiguously to the question of what goals they were striving for: they spoke in the categories of a 'happy' family life, with plans for a single-family house, a new car, a good education for the children and a rise in their own living standards. Today, people speak a different language, which necessarily circles vaguely around the search for identity and an individuality of one's own, with an objective of 'developing personal abilities' and 'remaining in motion'. This vagueness has both a personal and a social significance. In contrast to the traditional value system, where success could be unambiguously indicated (single-family house, car, etc.), no one today can really be certain when they have found what they are looking for and how they can communicate it reliably and convincingly to others. The consequence is that more and more people end up in the labyrinth of self-inflicted uncertainty, self-doubt and self-reassurance.

At the same time there is an infinite regression of questions: 'Am I really happy?', 'Am I really fulfilled?', 'Am I really doing what I want to do?', 'Who is speaking as "I" here, anyway?' This leads into one new 'response mode' after another, which can then be reforged in a variety of ways into markets for experts, industries and religious movements. In the search for fulfilment, people thus metamorphose under certain conditions into products of mass culture and mass consumption. Following the tourism catalogues, they travel into every corner of the world. They shatter the best marriages and soon thereafter enter into new unions.

They get retrained. They fast. They jog. They become activists. They switch from one therapy group to the next and swear at any given time by very diverse therapies and therapists. As self-assured as they might be, they continually discuss and explore their own uncertainties among themselves. Their complaining about the 'narcissism' of others serves to give more space to their own ego. Possessed by the goal of self-fulfilment, they tear themselves out of the ground just to see whether their own roots are really healthy (cf. Yankelovich 1979: 11f.).

This value system of individualization also contains starting points for a new ethics relying on the principle of 'duty to oneself'. For traditional ethics, this represents a complete contradiction, since 'duties' necessarily have a social character, harmonizing the deeds of the individual with the totality and tying him or her into it. These orientations can therefore easily be misunderstood as egocentric. Where they go beyond conventional notions of success, however, is in their orientation towards *self-liberation as process*, which includes the search and struggle for social ties and solidarity in the family, work and politics. This struggle is aimed at the freedom to avoid or overcome traditional role norms, and to try out new modes of behaviour and forms of coexistence, to express and give in to impulses and wishes that one was accustomed to suppress. It is focused on living out relationships, erotic and sexual needs, but also on the freedom to enjoy life now and not only in some distant future, and to develop and cultivate a 'culture of enjoyment' consciously and starting from scratch. It aims at the freedom to transform one's own needs into rights and turn them against institutional norms and obligations, the freedom to shield and protect one's own life against 'outside' interference, to provide it with a 'space of its own' (in the literal and the figurative sense) and to take social and political action wherever this space is threatened in a personally tangible manner.[12]

This deep-seated cultural erosion and evolution, of which we are the witnesses, has effects on attitudes to work on the one hand, and, on the other, it has direct consequences for the design and organization of work processes:

• In the wake of this evolution, primary and familial relationships are valued higher emotionally, while professional work is also given a higher value as a prerequisite of individual life conduct and as the central site for social and meaningful experience. The indifference assumption (Niklas Luhmann once said that a worker in a jam factory need not be fond of jam) becomes false; professionals begin to confront the (social) 'meaning' of their work, to identify with it or perhaps not. At the same time, what studies lump together under the generic term 'leisure time' is becoming more significant both objectively (reduction of working hours) and subjectively. Concealed behind this is quite obviously the 'realization of a life of one's own', no longer exclusively or predominantly conceived of in the categories of familial life from the 1950s, with everything that entails.[13] In this way, the realization of a life of one's own begins to burst the bonds of private family life and to extend into the grey areas between politics and the public sphere (as is becoming visible in the rise of citizens' initiatives, group work, communal work, new types of neighbourhoods and so on).

• Women are released from their bonds to marital and familial existence and, as an expression of this development, 'working for money' achieves an essential *symbolic significance* for individual self-affirmation and self-discovery, alongside the economic security it offers.

• Whereas in the old value system, the person fuses together with his or her occupation (and suffers considerably from this), personal identity is now beginning to free itself from the occupational role, or at least to behave more independently of it. If people formerly answered the question 'What are you?' self-evidently, 'I'm a secretary, a technician, a teacher, a businessman, a shopkeeper' and so forth, thus directly equating person and profession, the answers today, under the influence of the new value orientations, come out more hesitantly and with more differentiation: 'I'm . . . Well, what am I? I am certainly a secretary, but above all, I am a person with my own interests and hopes and an "identity under construction" *beyond* my occupation.'

• Surprisingly, old and new value systems converge in the symbolic significance that paid labour has for the members of our society. This is clear for the traditional value system, where occupational success is the prerequisite for masculine self-affirmation in work as well as in marital and familial life. The central concern of individualization revolves around convincing people that all options for self-fulfilment must be kept open. To this end, even already established commitments (marriage or occupation) may be dissolved if necessary. One of the essential prerequisites for this, however, is economic security, which still means, alongside property and welfare state protections, the availability of an income of one's own from paid labour. Individualization thus *intensifies* the dependence of the individual on paid and wage labour and this insight should become more rather than less accepted in the wake of individualization processes.[14] This implies, however, that following the cultural evolution being described here, one can count on a *quantitative increase of desire for employment along with its simultaneous diversification and individualization*.[15] 'Automating jobs out of existence' thus coincides in a single generation with a culturally conditioned growth in the demand for jobs, and this is likely to intensify the problem of unemployment in the future even further.

• This growing interest in paid labour should not conceal the fact that the willingness to expend labour power is changing at the same time. Participation in paid labour is the prerequisite for leading a life 'of one's own', for complying with and pursuing 'obligations' to oneself and demands for self-discovery; of course, it also leads to the constriction and constraints of routine, controlled industrial and office work. Under the influence of the new value orientations, therefore, it is becoming more probable that a person may take on a paid job and simultaneously attempt to circumvent the disciplinary performance expectations of enterprises and supervisors. While the pay is the prerequisite for ensuring access to 'self-realization', the expenditure of one's labour power no longer necessarily follows the traditional 'professional obligations', but neither is it simply a 'job orientation'. Instead it becomes dependent on the fulfilment of *substantive* expectations: opportunities for individual and social development in the work, the 'point' one finds in doing it and the 'fun' in it. This learning process and change of orientation may be concealed or scaled back under conditions of recession and mass unemployment; it continues to be promoted, however, by the social safety network, the expansion of education and the public discussions of threats to the future inflicted by civilization. Wherever demands for development are transferred to wage labour, the 'dual-purpose structure' of wage labour – the coupling of payment and performance – disintegrates more clearly even for the working people.[16] Opportunities to circumvent controls or 'instrumentalize' them for one's own purposes are explored and expanded; highly developed and highly sensitive technologies offer additional starting points for this.

• In the wake of individualization processes, certain serious drawbacks in the remuneration system as it now exists thus become clearer and clearer. It is uniform where it should be diversified; even there it relies primarily on economic controls at a time when these are less and less effective in activating the willingness and the morale for achievement. Management and enterprises (both private and public), moreover, often misunderstand the quality and deep structure of the new cultural developments and orientations, demonize them as 'declining performance' and react with intensified monitoring and standardization, instead of with a liberalization of labour standards.

• Aside from a few pilot projects, the organizational plans of companies, the structure of labour agreements and the regulation of working hours and conditions all proceed from the assumption that *everyone* has *the same* demands, needs and orientations in regard to work, precisely those which are dictated by the rhythm of the machines, the sequence of production processes and the organization's plans.[17] Individuality must be left at home or checked in at the door. The system of industrial labour is at its core a system of control and standardization. Despite a number of loosening tendencies (the 'cultivation' of informal relationships, humanization projects and regulations for worker consultation), it is still largely immune to the diversity of cultural demands. Thus it is misunderstood or goes unnoticed that while some people are primarily interested in money, others would prefer compensation in leisure time. Some seek opportunities for advancement and others are primarily interested in concrete satisfaction from the work objective itself or in its communicative significance, interaction with people. All of this in turn changes, depending on the type of work, the demographical composition and the local subculture. Informally, the corresponding 'individualization of labour and employment conditions' is conceded to a certain extent (particularly in small operations and to management itself); formally, however, people insist on the standardized employment and remuneration structure. Naturally, the reason for this is the convenience of administering and organizing such a structure. Attempts to respond flexibly to this cultural diversity of demands easily fail when they meet signs of the organizational and bureaucratic complexity it provokes. As a result, these problems still go largely unnoticed in personnel divisions and management. This was possible under the old value system because the game of 'carrot and stick' still worked. Under the new system, people take the carrot and attempt to avoid the stick. This may still be covered up by the 'disciplinary effect' of real or threatening unemployment. In the future, however, management, and the trade unions as well, will have to face up to this cultural and social reality (see below for more detail).

• An additional shortcoming is the clinging to the dominance of economic remuneration, which completely ignores the broad spectrum of new needs and orientations, at a time where what can be bought with money counts less and less in terms of status value and more and more in terms of use value. Under these conditions, 'financial success' loses its motivating power, at least if it must be purchased by sacrificing what individuals have learned to understand as 'self-development' and as self-respect. This is concealed in part by the losses of real income which working people have had to put up with in the past years in circumstances of high inflation and low increases in wages. At the same time, there is a 'revenge effect' here, paradoxically enough. Wherever the demands for appreciation and self-development on the job are violated, the employees demand a compensatory increase in wages. This in turn misleads management to the false conclusion that the meaning of money for the employees has increased, although in fact it is decreasing under the influence of the new value orientations, and the increased demands can also be interpreted as reactions to the inflexibility of management.

In this sense, the breakthrough of the new wave of cultural individualization into the world of work is often misunderstood and underestimated by employers today, and even where people are beginning to re-learn, there is a belief that these new cultural trends and value orientations are incompatible with the requirements for efficiency and productivity. Why should this not be possible at our present level of technical and organizational development? In the ideal case, people shaped by these trends want to work in small groups where they can develop close ties to others. Many would like more personal responsibility and independence from outside control; they also want to learn and experience new things at work; they want to deal with others in their work and to be able to identify themselves with it and its products. Should technology, of all things, which has opened the way to the moon for us, really be able to prevent us from doing the obvious thing, for instance, introducing a de-anonymization of industrial firms, administrative apparatuses and state bureaucracies, indeed a transformation of the latter into 'villages'? Perhaps a new generation of managers, engineers and organizers must first grow up in the firms, a generation which is itself shaped by the new cultural orientations and expectations, before it will be recognized that this cultural evolution of work is not only technically and organizationally possible, but even *productivity enhancing*, within the overall conditions of the new value system.

Of course, this speculation about a new managerial generation is definitely not a guarantee of a corresponding change in the employment and organization of labour. Rather, the tendencies for intraorganizational change and the learning process already coming into view are more likely to be of importance in the future. Under the influence of exactly these new value orientations (which, looked at another way, after all, also represent novel sales and marketing opportunities) and also in view of the impending sweeping technological and economic developments (in the fields of microelectronics and communications media, for instance), the firms are coming under permanent *pressure to innovate*, which will force them sooner or later to revise Taylorist forms of rationalization and labour *for reasons of cost*. The detailed planning and monitoring of production and work processes drastically restricts the flexibility of the firms, which may be crucial to competitiveness, and causes immense costs which could be shifted to well-trained employees by taking advantage of greater self-initiative, scope for collective action and awareness of problems. A corresponding learning process is becoming noticeable today even in the former centres of Taylorism, the highly automated assembly divisions of mass-production industry:

> Even if these remain manual labour jobs in the future, despite rapidly accelerated assembly machines (more and more accomplished assembly robots), the range of working capabilities called upon will become broader here as well. As a result of the increasing complexity and variability of the products in response to the market, a broader variety of operations will be demanded of the individual worker. Repetitive division of labour no longer means doing the same thing in every cycle. Moreover, serious consideration is also being given in assembly work as to whether the old principles such as 'blind obedience rather than individual reflection' . . . really yield optimal performance (reduction of inspections or 'quality circles' as concrete experiments).[18]

Pointing in the same direction are reflections, following up on Orio Giarni, which start from the view that the risks from, vulnerability to and resistance against megatechnologies grow as the threats to the future from civilization become more scientific in nature, and thus the economic utility of such technologies declines.[19] If the *returns from technology diminish*, the firms must seek ways to solve problems of productivity by recourse to other sources of productivity, that is, social and management innovations: 'new ways for employees to participate in the planning, implementation and returns of their work; new management strategies that remove the weaknesses of previous industrial technology – concentration and vulnerability – by decentralization and autonomy of smaller units' (Zapf 1983: 298). An example:

> A few years ago [a large Japanese company] took over a factory from [an American company] near Chicago and began producing television sets there. The company kept its 1,000 production workers but dismissed half of the 600 supervisors and managers. In two years, production doubled and the customer complaint rate fell from 60 per cent to 4 per cent. In addition, the company reduced its annual warranty replacement costs from 14 million to 2 million by better quality control . . . The whole theory is this: workers know their jobs better than anyone else and if they have the opportunity, they will be creative and self-motivated. (ibid.)

Of course, this example also shows that, alongside the replacement of jobs by technological systems and the culturally determined increase in demand for jobs in the wake of individualization processes, this type of *social innovation and 'management rationalization'* can lead to a considerable growth of unemployment in the future and hence to an exacerbation of the resulting political problems.

5

Capitalism without Work, or the Coming of Civil Society

'So: tell me about yourself!' At a dinner party in the suburbs, skewered. lamb cooking on the grill, the conversational tone flippant, the answer to this question is no longer framed in terms of a hobby, a sign of the Zodiac, or a profession; nowadays, being unemployed has become a conversation topic. You can run into anyone down at the unemployment office; class distinctions no longer hold.

The members of the professional elite are doing their best to preserve an ironic attitude towards the absurdities and humiliations of the job search. A teacher regales her listeners with the story of how she was told at the unemployment office to sign up for the course on 'How to apply for a job' that she herself was offering not long ago. A biologist with years of research experience brings tears of laughter to the eyes of his audience, mimicking the personnel director who just interviewed him, solecisms, inappropriate questions and all. Then comes the point of the story: sorry, he's overqualified.

Insecurity on the labour market has long since spread beyond the 'lower classes'. It has become the mark of our times. The old 'lifetime profession' is threatened with extinction. No one wants to admit that with it an entire value system, a society based on gainful employment, will disappear.

Capitalism is killing off work. Unemployment no longer afflicts only those on the margin; it has the potential to strike all of us, and to put democracy as a way of life at risk. But as global capitalism divests itself of all responsibility for employment and for democracy, it is undermining its own legitimacy. Before a new Marx comes along to wake up the West, we had better dig up some fresh ideas and models as the basis for a revised social contract. We have to lay the groundwork for democracy in a post-work society.

An example: in that promised land of employment, Great Britain, only a third of the able-bodied population is still employed in the classic sense – full-time, long-term, benefits guaranteed. In Germany, to be sure, the figure is still more than 60 per cent. Only 20 years ago it was more than 80 per cent in both countries. The heralded cure, of making employment flexible, has merely covered over and prolonged the disease of unemployment; it has done nothing to cure it. On the contrary, the disease is spreading: unemployment and the confusing new phenomenon of part-time work, employment without security, and the still quiescent pool of surplus labour. We are headed for capitalism without work in all the postindustrial countries.

Three myths prevent those engaged in the public debate from recognizing the true state of affairs. First, the impenetrability myth: everything is just too complicated, the economy is beyond our understanding. Second, the service myth: the imminent upswing in the service economy will come to the rescue of the work-based society. Third, the labour-cost myth: all we have to do is get labour costs down to rock bottom and the problem of unemployment will solve itself.

That everything is connected with everything else (however loosely) and is therefore impenetrable can certainly be said of developments on the labour market in an era of forced globalization. This does not, however, invalidate statements about secular trends, as demonstrated by the comparative international longitudinal studies that Meinhard Miegel presented to the Bavarian and Saxon Commission on the Future at its last conference in Dresden. According to Miegel, over the course of many generations the value of work kept going up. In the mid-1970s a turning point was reached. Since then, gainful employment has been perceptibly shrinking everywhere, either directly through unemployment (as in Germany) or concealed behind exponentially growing 'motley forms of employment' (as in the United States and Great Britain). The demand for work is declining, the supply of labour rising (also as a result of globalization). Indicators for a precipitous decline in gainful employment have reached the alarm stage.

We have long since moved from redistributing work to redistributing unemployment – this, too, disguised in the new forms of temporary, unskilled, part-time work. This holds true even for those so-called employment paradises, the United States and Great Britain, where growing numbers subsist in the twilight zone between work and no work, often making do with starvation wages.

Politicians and business leaders still think in the fictitious categories of full employment. Even savings banks and insurance companies offer loans and mortgages and underwrite policies on the assumption that people who are 'employed' have a long-term guaranteed income. The rapidly spreading neither–nor situation, neither unemployed nor with a secure income, hardly fits this stereotype. Yet we still bemoan 'massive unemployment', assuming that a person's natural condition from adulthood to retirement is full-time work.

Many believe, hope and pray that the service economy will save us from the devouring monster of unemployment. This is the myth of service jobs. The calculations and countercalculations have yet to be tested. New jobs will certainly be created. But first the opposite will occur: the traditionally secure core of jobs in the service sector will be swept away in a wave of automation that is just beginning to gather strength. Telebanking, for instance, will result in the closing of many branch banks; telecommunications will eliminate about 60,000 jobs in Germany alone; entire professions, like that of secretary, may disappear altogether. And even the new jobs that do spring up can be located just about anywhere. Many companies, of which American Express is a recent example, set up entire administrative divisions in countries with low wages, in this case South India.

The prophets of the information society who predicted a surplus of highly paid jobs even for people with minimal skills were wrong. The sobering fact is that even many of the jobs in data processing will be poorly paid and boring. US Secretary of Labor Robert Reich writes that data processors sitting in back rooms at computer terminals hooked up to worldwide databanks are the foot soldiers of the information economy.

Labour costs

The illusion that occupies the key position in the current debate is the myth of labour costs. More and more people are succumbing to the often vehemently asserted conviction that only a radical reduction in labour costs and wages will lead us out of the vale of unemployment. Here the 'American way' shines like a beacon.

But if we compare the United States with Germany, it turns out that the American 'jobs miracle' is a mixed phenomenon. New jobs for highly trained workers that are both secure and well paid are being created neither more nor less frequently than in a top-wage country like Germany; that is, at a rate of 2.6 per cent, according to figures supplied in April 1996 by the Organization for Economic Cooperation and Development. The difference between the two countries can be found in the growth of poorly paid unskilled jobs. But a comparison of productivity also takes the mystery out of the American 'solution'. In the last 20 years, productivity in the United States has increased by only 25 per cent, whereas in Germany it has risen a full 100 per cent. 'How in the world do the Germans do it?' an American colleague asked me recently. 'They work so much less and produce so much more.'

Here we have the new law of productivity that global capitalism in the information age has discovered: fewer and fewer well-trained and globally interchangeable people can generate more and more output and services. Thus economic growth no longer reduces unemployment but actually requires a reduction in the number of jobs.

Let there be no illusion: a capitalism focused only on ownership and profits, which turns its back on the employed, on the social welfare state and on democracy, will undermine itself. While the profit margins of the multinational corporations are growing, these same companies are stripping the high-priced countries of both jobs and tax revenue. Two chronically impoverished sources, public funds and the private funds of those who are still employed, are supposed to pay for everything the rich also continue to enjoy: schools and universities with sophisticated facilities, smoothly functioning transportation systems, environmental protection, safe roads, the wealth of opportunities afforded by urban living.

Democracy in Europe and the United States was originally a 'democracy of work', in the sense that it rested on participation in gainful employment. Citizens had to earn their keep in one way or another in order to give content to their freedoms. Work for pay always formed the basis not only for private but also for political existence. So what is now at risk is not 'merely' millions without work. Not 'merely' the social welfare state, or the prevention of poverty, or the possibility of justice. Political freedom and Western democracy are at risk.

The connection that exists in the West between capitalism and basic political, social and economic rights is far more than a mere 'social benefit' that can be dispensed with when things get tight. Rather, socially buffered capitalism was a response to the experience of fascism and the challenge of communism, a response developed at no small cost. This form of capitalism represents the enlightened recognition that only when people have a decent place to live and a secure job can they function as citizens who embrace democracy and make it come alive. The truth is simple: without material security, no political freedom. And no democracy – which in turn leaves people at the mercy of old and new totalitarian regimes and ideologies.

We must beat it into the heads of these pseudo-free democrats or free pseudo-democrats, who turn a deaf ear to historical experience, that the market fundamentalism they idolize is a form of democratic illiteracy.

What the market precisely does not do is provide its own justification. This form of economy can survive only in conjunction with material security, social rights, and democracy. Anyone who relies solely on the market destroys democracy and along with it this form of economy.

Today, the only serious opponent of capitalism is . . . capitalism based exclusively on profit. Disastrous tidings on the employment front are hailed as victories on Wall Street. The underlying arithmetic is easy to see: when labour costs fall, profits go up. Yet the contradictions of 'jobless capitalism' are becoming apparent. The directors of multinational corporations ship administrative functions off to South India but send their own children to the great publicly financed universities of Europe. It would never occur to them to move to the places where they are creating low-paying jobs and paying low corporate taxes.

Without a moment's hesitation they lay claim to the costly political, social and civil rights whose public financing they are torpedoing. They go to the theatre. They enjoy expensively maintained open space. They frolic in the still relatively crime- and violence-free capitals of Europe. But at the same time they are contributing, through their egotistic economic behaviour and their profit-oriented policies, to the destruction of this European way of life. May we ask where they or their children intend to live when the costs of maintaining the democratic state can no longer be met?

Public work

In the old industrial society, two 'employers' occupied the dominant position: capital and the state. In the future, both will be chronically absent in this function. Capitalism is creating joblessness and will more and more be jobless. To call the public coffers 'empty' is more than an understatement. We have the choice of wailing about that or creating a new focus of activity and identity that will revitalize the democratic way of life: 'public work'. If public discourse is the art of involving strangers in a continuing discussion of what affects them most intimately, public work is the art of making deeds follow the words. So what does this concept imply?

First, active compassion: environmental activists in Germany are motivated by fear of destruction and deterioration, but even more by indignation at the thoughtless way in which most people behave. Active resistance to indifference has many goals and many faces: work with the elderly and the handicapped, with the homeless and with AIDS patients, with illiterates and the excluded; with women's centres, Greenpeace,

Amnesty International and so forth. 'Public work' in this sense means an odd blend of politics, care for others and everyday cooperation.

Second, practical critique: many lawyers, tax consultants, physicians, businesspeople and administrators want to use their professional skills in different settings for a change, exerting influence over public opinion and legislation, devising economic strategies for self-help groups, providing information on avoiding tax liability, advising people on handling debt, calling attention to health and safety risks, and so on. Why not establish prizes and awards for such forms of civil resistance? (Of course, citizens should be the ones to award them.)

Third, active democracy: citizen participation and decentralization. In the administration of many cities and communities, a small cultural revolution has broken out. It promises to bring not only greater efficiency but also a gain in democracy. 'All these citizen initiatives just duplicate existing governmental bodies,' a city council officer grumbles. But that is precisely the point: people acquire a taste for democracy by practising it. Freedom begets, strengthens and expands freedom.

What all this means is that we have to invest in civil society. We have to delegate power and authority to it, and in every respect: technologically (information media), economically (basic investment), educationally (certification that will be valid on the labour market as well).

How do the values and goals of an earnings-based society relate to the grass-roots organization of civil society? The relationship is one not of mutual exclusion but of complementarity. In the future, what will probably win out is a blending of formal work and voluntary organization, the dismantling of legal and mobility barriers between the two sectors, the creation of opportunities for leaving or changing one's principal occupation (in an annual, monthly or weekly rhythm). Two things would thus become possible. First, the equation of public activity with remunerated employment would be broken. Second, public work would create new foci of political action and identity formation within and opposed to a fragmented society. The material and cultural foundations for 'individualism coupled with solidarity' would be established.

Four objections will serve to sharpen this apparently simple idea and show how it can be turned into a viable reality. First: won't public work come to grief the moment it encounters the selfishness that has overrun our society? Second: who is supposed to pay for this? Third: is such a thing possible under conditions of globalization? Fourth: won't 'creative unemployment' (Ivan Illich's term) make people unhappy? Doesn't identity crumble when gainful employment is taken away?

Let's look first at the much maligned 'selfish society'. The American sociologist Robert Wuthnow has shown that without voluntary efforts dedicated to others, all modern societies would collapse immediately. Eighty million Americans, or 45 per cent of those above the age of 18, commit five hours or more, week after week, to helping others or working for charitable purposes. The monetary value of these efforts amounts to about 150 billion dollars a year.

This study also shows that for 75 per cent of the American population, solidarity, helpfulness and concern for the general welfare are as important as self-actualization, professional success and expansion of personal freedom. The notion of the 'selfish society' assumes that two things are mutually exclusive that in fact belong together: self-actualization and being there for others.

That the situation is any different in Europe can be believed only by those who confuse commitment with membership in organizations. Although young people are staying away in droves from organized churches, parties, unions and associations, private initiatives of all sorts are attracting participants in record numbers. According to a poll of European Community countries, these same young people who shun the tedium of collective organizations express strong support (over 80 per cent) for environmental causes; 73 per cent see homelessness as a major issue and want to do something about it personally; 71 per cent demand more rights for the handicapped; 71 per cent support feminism and see it as important for both men and women.

As for the decline in values and the growth of indifference among young people, a trend already bemoaned by Plato, these too are connected to a 'blockage of institutional commitments'. Young people are given rights, but citizen initiatives are more and more hemmed in by governmental restrictions. Power is not really delegated; many are reluctant to get involved because they have already found that 'nothing comes of it'.

Who pays?

Who is supposed to finance investment in 'social capital' in an active society? In Germany we have over 4 trillion marks in private household accounts, very unequally distributed. Ten per cent of all households account for a good 49 per cent of the wealth; 40 per cent of households for the next 49 per cent; 50 per cent of households have only 2.4 per cent of all private wealth.

The entrepreneurs have discovered the mother lode. Their new magic formula goes this way: capitalism without work plus capitalism without taxes. Revenue from the corporation tax, the tax on company profits, fell between 1989 and 1993 by 18.6 per cent; its share in the total tax revenue was cut almost in half (from 6.4 to 3.7 per cent), while at the same time profits rose by more than 10 per cent. These data reveal, among other things, the new power relationships created by globalization. Many companies are becoming taxpayers only in principle, not in fact.

Capital is globally mobile; nation-states, on the other hand, have to stay put. When the manufacture of a product is spread over several countries and continents, it becomes increasingly difficult to assign the profit to a specific locale; at the same time, strategies whereby companies can undermine the tax system become easier to implement.

The internationalization of production gives companies two strategic advantages: global competition springs up between expensive and inexpensive labour, and the tax structures and monitoring systems of various countries can be played off against each other and subverted. In the new-found power of the multinational corporations we can observe the successful application of the laws of the free market to the political realm. In reality, however, the situation is much more dicey. Since utilization of numerous social resources (expensive universities, hospitals, transportation systems, the courts, research funds) is not restricted to the place where taxes are assessed, many corporations are in a position to minimize their tax burden while establishing their headquarters in the countries that maintain the best infrastructures.

The sites of investment, production, taxation and residence can now be completely uncoupled from one another. Once again, business leaders take advantage of the low tax rates of the poor countries while enjoying the high standard of living found in the rich countries. They pay taxes where it is cheapest and live where conditions are most appealing. This situation carries considerable potential for social conflict. First of all, tension arises between virtual and real taxpayers, that is, those individuals who still have work and the smaller companies that are not in a position to move and thereby escape regular taxation. These are the losers in the globalization game.

Then, too, it is precisely the champions of economic growth, assiduously wooed by the politicians, who are undermining the authority of the state by taking advantage of its offerings while snatching away its revenues. These new virtuosi of virtual taxation are subverting the general welfare in a legal but illegitimate fashion, and along with it political life and the democratic state. Neoliberal policies, which uncritically embrace the free market, have much in common with those proponents of efficiency in business who make themselves superfluous.

There is only one conclusion to be drawn: we must break the taboo on speaking of this new social injustice. Those who profit from globalization must be made accountable for the general welfare. Our system of social welfare needs reforming in many respects, but paradoxically the answer is not less but more money, properly invested and distributed! For investments in public works the watchword is: a little goes a long way. Society flourishes, public wealth grows.

Here it becomes clear that we need a new definition of 'wealth'. Among other things, this definition must include such indicators as social participation and political freedom. For a society whose economy is flourishing while putting people out of work is not a 'rich' society but only a rump society for the rich.

Who is supposed to pay for this? Let me propose three speculative models.

Model 1 Tax abatement. Here those who contribute to the general welfare must be allowed to pay substantially lower taxes (as individuals can already deduct contributions and charitable organizations can claim tax-exempt status). Objection: at the level of household income, this model is predicated on wage-bearing work. Those who are already earning well will be given the opportunity to enrich their lives through public commitment.

Model 2 Tax-financed basic support payment. Here those who participate in voluntary organizations receive a sort of 'public stipend' (as has already been partially implemented in Saxony). If the 'American model' results in a combination of full employment and growth in the number of the working poor, the 'German (European) model' could have as its goal a combination of wage-earning work and state-financed participation in civil society. Those who commit themselves to voluntary organizations are no longer 'available for the labour market' and in this sense are no longer 'unemployed'. They are active citizens who get involved on behalf of the general welfare and receive in return (time-limited) basic support payments.

Model 3 Citizens' support for all, financed through taxation; the appropriate amount is open to discussion. Many fear that this type of basic support will permanently stereotype and exclude from jobs and society those most at risk: women, the poor, the disabled. It would thus be essential not to pay out citizens' support in cold cash, but to link it with opportunities for active participation suitable for an inclusive society.

Can such a millennial reform be instituted in a single country? If the basic diagnosis offered here is correct, that capitalism is becoming jobless and is creating joblessness, we are dealing with a global challenge that will sooner or later confront all highly developed societies. But the country that first finds a practicable response, that meets the risks to democracy head-on, will be ahead of the game (economically as well).

As for the alleged monopoly that gainful employment has on identity formation, empirical studies have already shown that a far-reaching change of attitude is underway: more and more people are looking for both meaningful work and opportunities for commitment outside of work. If society can upgrade and reward such commitment and put it on a level with gainful employment, it can create both individual identity and social cohesion.

The scenario I have sketched here can be summed up in a plea to take the invisible practice of social self-help and grass-roots political organization and make it visible; give it economic, organizational and political weight. This becomes possible only if we invest in civil society, thereby democratizing democracy, so to speak. What we need is a citizen-state alliance for civil society, if need be in opposition to work and capital. But this alliance should attract all those who hold democracy dear.

6

The Democratization of the Family, or the Unknown Art of Free Association

It might be suggested that this title confuses and confounds apples and oranges, political and private, the rights and obligations of the citizen and the intimacy of the family. In a conventional view of modernity, which equates it with industrial society and prescribes the latter into the future, despite modernity's dynamism, this is indeed apparent. Those theories cultivate and make into a theoretical absolute the image of separate system worlds, each obeying certain mutually exclusive 'logics' (communicative codes). In theories of a second, reflexive modernity, where globalization and individualization processes occupy the centre of attention, this either–or organizational scheme becomes untenable. It is replaced by problems of 'and'. One can characterize this second modernity by the fact that codes of behaviour which permeate it have previously been considered separate. This can be shown in a great many topics and fields, including, as is our intention in this chapter, in the interpenetration of civil freedom and family.

For sociology, this implies that the dynamism of political freedom must be considered a core dynamism of modernity, which in a contradictory mixture of competition with and parallelism to other fundamental dynamisms emphasized by sociologists, such as functional differentiation, the exploitation of capital, rationalization and bureaucratization, is changing the bases for action in modern society in an evolutionary fashion. This view, this theory of the second modernity, comprises questions and conjectures that, in turn, contain thousands of hypotheses of current changes and their interpretations in almost all fields of social action. Picking out the example of our topic, cannot the indicators of radical change in the family, such as high divorce rates, declining numbers of children, extramarital ways of life, mothers working outside the home and so on, also be interpreted in keeping with our title as a 'democratization of the family'? Might this not even be a compromise between those who claim to be able to discern dissolution in the data and those who claim to be able to read a constancy of familial structure from the same data? Doesn't the family (and quite similarly the churches, political parties, trade unions and organizations) reveal the break-up of traditional structures of dependency and authority that typically goes hand in hand with taking advantage of freedoms (and with all the same conflicts, dilemmas and decay of order)? And would not this view, finally, result in directing the attention of the sociology of the family towards the internal conditions even of 'intact' families (viewed superficially in terms of statistical indicators) and no longer only towards the deviations from whatever is simply assumed to be a 'family', in the broadest sense, as part of an attempted refutation of a misunderstood theory of individualization? And anticipating a final question, would it not be necessary in this context to take up a now-forgotten tradition of the sociology of the family, that is to say, the enquiry into the connections between authority and family, which was once central to the early Frankfurt School, just before their emigration? Are their assumptions still valid, or are they becoming false with the break-up of traditional authority relationships in the family; with new and possibly problematic consequences?

The same question could be posed for the authority relationships in industrial plants, in the service sector, in schools, churches, political parties and organizations. Perhaps we are involved everywhere in an uprising for greater freedom? And perhaps we are all illiterate in the art and language of fostering, crafting and protecting relationships voluntarily?

Schematically and tentatively, two arguments are sketched out in this programmatic context: first, some definitions and distinctions regarding the sociology of political freedom, which would also have to become the sociology of citizenship (if it were ever fully articulated); second, this will be applied to families, particularly to the situation of (women and) children. Some concluding remarks will tie that back up with the introduction.

The uncomprehended freedom: on the sociology of the citizen

In German there is one poet to whom the honorary title of 'poet of freedom' attaches more than any other, Friedrich Schiller, and in one of his dramas there is the famous quotation: 'Sire, grant freedom for thoughts!' This comes from his drama *Don Carlos*, and the words are spoken ('with ardour', as the stage direction puts it) by the Marquis Posa to the King of Spain (although a king of Prussia is probably intended).

The very demand for freedom for thoughts is absurd. Thoughts are free, according to the folksong: 'No one can guess them / They fly past like shades of night.' The meaning of political and civil freedoms is the exact opposite in every detail. Such freedoms can neither be begged for from the kindness or grace of the ruler nor granted by him or her; they must be seized by the citizens. Citizens do not get down on their knees to achieve something that is missed, even betrayed by genuflection, namely, freedom. Instead, the freely formulated decision of citizens is what makes democratically legitimated power and rule possible.

Freedom of will vs political freedom

From this, one can derive an initial but essential distinction. The debate in Germany has been under the spell of philosophical idealism and its understanding of freedom as an inner freedom, a freedom of the will (or a *transcendental* freedom). By contrast, the concept of political freedom, referring to law, parliament, the public sphere and so on, remained pale and dim. In the 'new' social movements of the 1970s and 1980s, such as the women's movement, but also in the many citizens' initiative groups and in the struggles for ecological ways of life and lifestyles, there were experiments from the early days on with the unification of both traditions and concepts of freedom: self-realization inwardly and outwardly. Yet this remained oddly inconsequential for the public comprehension of freedom in Germany. It is not an exaggeration to say that the debate on freedom there is still attuned to an idealism with, by now, therapeutic functions.

The early and major exception is Hannah Arendt, who never tired of demonstrating that 'freedom is an essentially political phenomenon, that it is experienced primarily neither in volition nor in thought, but rather in activity and is thus dependent on a political space prepared for this activity' which 'contradicts very old and very venerable ideas':

> Neither the philosophical concept of freedom, reaching back to late antiquity, for which freedom is a phenomenon of thought, nor the Christian and modern freedom of the will is political in nature. Indeed, both contain a decidedly antipolitical position which, for its part, is by no means a figment of philosophers' imaginations . . . rather, it refers back to highly authentic experiences which people have had with politics . . . For us,

it must suffice to remember the near-unanimous response of tradition to our question regarding the relationship of freedom and politics: freedom begins only where a person has withdrawn from living with the multitude, i.e., the political sphere, and he experiences freedom in interaction with himself, not with others, either in dialogue with himself, which we have identified with thinking ever since Socrates, or in conflict with himself, in the conflict of volition and ability, in which Christianity, following Paul and Augustine, saw the insufficiency and dubiousness of human freedom. (Arendt 1958)

Freedom as idea and condition

Even on the side of political freedom we do not wish to get carried off into false idealizations and get lost there. Therefore a second distinction is essential, namely that between freedom as *idea* and as social *reality*. It is not difficult to recall that the rights everyone talks about, rights to resistance, challenges to civil courage and so on, need not have anything to do with what is actually the case and is actually happening and what will be enforced by state power if need be. Often it can even be observed that the enunciation of rights, the rhetoric and myth of freedom, is intended precisely to cover up their severe abridgement. Where rights to freedom merely adorn the preamble to the constitution, which no one can read anyway because the public is subject to officially decreed political illiteracy, there can be no serious discussion of the social reality of civil rights.

Here too, however, there exists the possibility, no matter how slight, of taking the rhetoric of freedom literally. That means that freedom, even in its watered-down form, is effective and real even as an *idea*, perhaps only in negative form, specifically in the arming of state power to make sure that the idea of freedom, now culturally internalized, is not able to strike a political spark.

If one wishes not to lose sight of the political power of the pure idea, it makes sense to introduce another distinction, namely, that between potential and actual freedom (in a given society, at a given time and a given place). It is certainly correct that everywhere in the world, including societies which have inscribed human rights on their banners, the social reality is that women are excluded from actually participating in the freedoms granted them on paper. But, conversely, no one can fail to see that just this contradiction between claim and reality always develops a hard-to-control subversive effect, at least latently. Even where the response is the impatience of the victims, this impatience and the policy of contestation in which it expresses itself are often nourished from the surreptitiously smouldering contradiction between the potentiality and the reality of freedom.

The legal form and the social form of freedom

The distinction between idea and reality, between effective potential and the actual social condition of freedom must be supplemented and made more concrete by another distinction, that between rights to freedom as a category of law and rights to freedom as a category of the thought and action of individuals, that is, society. At first sight one might believe that this marks the boundary between questions of law and those of the social sciences. That is not the case, however. Freedom is present as both a legal category and a category of consciousness in the enquiries of social scientists just as much as in those of jurists. Even social scientists wonder whether certain fundamental rights can be enforced or how they will be interpreted in the courts at the various levels of jurisprudential practice. Yet there can scarcely be any doubt that social researchers devote special attention to the question of how rights to freedom are represented and refracted in the consciousness, self-consciousness and actions of groups. This distinction is necessary for a central reason: the questions of the legal constitution and the social constitution of civil liberties can neither be reflected by one another nor derived from one another. In other words, there exists a relationship of relative independence between the two which it is important to comprehend.

Precisely in the historical comprehension of the importance of legal conditions, it is often insinuated that political freedoms are possible only where there is a government under the rule of law. The fallacy in this assumption can be revealed and understood by the very simple fact that if it were true, there could never have been the rebellion of human rights advocates against the tyrannical system in the communist Eastern bloc, to cite one example. In that case, people demanded the fundamental rights due them, defying the state-sanctioned legal apparatus, and thus ultimately helped bring down the unjust system which had codified itself in law. To link political freedoms exclusively or too tightly to the prior existence of a law-based government is not only to misunderstand the political efficacy of the idea of freedom, which can be demanded and seized at any moment; it also denies any real political power to all the civil rights and freedom movements in dictatorships of all kinds, and strips resistance, possible everywhere and anywhere, of its dignity.

One can also view the same state of affairs from the other side. Even in the most perfect governments drawn up under the rule of law, with constitutions which transform fairy-tale books of political freedoms into rights of pure gold, freedoms can fall asleep or doze. Rights to freedom favour but do not guarantee the social reality and vitality of freedoms. Rather, the latter remain tied exclusively to the concrete actions of people, their fantasy, impatience and initiative, their courage, doubt and long-lasting anger, even if the ultimate legal authority, the constitution, proclaims a guarantee of these freedoms. Indeed, it is even possible that in the self-satisfied rejoicing over the miraculous power of the constitution, one may postpone, or forget, the necessary conflict over how and with what concrete objectives and institutions it is to be filled out and given life and structure.

Two intellectual tendencies can therefore be distinguished, each attempting to demonstrate in its own way the inner connection between politics, freedom and individual action: *intuitionism* on the one hand, and *institutionalism* on the other. In the former, everything good comes from the inside, from self-reflection, while in the latter, everything good comes from the law (constitution) in force. In both paths it is easy to lose sight of the fact that freedom is indeed only colourful and powerful to the extent that it is constantly being fought for and remade in the co-operative and confrontational action of individuals who are aware of freedom.

The question of the spirit of democracy

But that does not exhaust the distinction between the legal form and the social form of political freedoms. This is evident when the question is raised: how does the spirit of freedom become the spirit of an entire society, or fail to do so? How do freedom and democracy become not just ways of government but ways of life?

No one will deny that courts, codes of law or parliamentary committees are important institutions and products (protectors) of democracy or that the demolition of fundamental rights sets off loud alarms. But the jungle of legal provisions and the subtleties of juridical thinking and decision-making are by no means identical to the spirit of freedom and political action. For one thing, this means that democracy remains a matter for experts, that is to say, *technocracy*. Furthermore, the juridical understanding of freedom, institutionalism, is always in danger of confusing the letter of the law, the legal text (the *Bundesgesetzblatt*, the Federal Law Journal), with social reality. Precisely when looking at the spirit of democracy, which fills out or inspires an entire society, it must be said that the mere one-sided legal conception of freedom tends towards legal authoritarianism. This is indeed a step on from absolutist forms of rule, but it remains stuck part way by bureaucratically dessicating or choking off the spirit of freedom, under the banners of democratic rights to freedom, accompanied by the fanfares of grandiose constitutional promises.

The therapeutic and democratic self

If one takes the other point of view, changing, that is, from the legal to the social understanding of rights to freedom, then there is no obvious reason to equate and confuse the democratization of a society with its governance by laws. It is possible here to distinguish two ways of making the spirit of democracy the spirit of a society: one is by *socialization* (schools, universities, parental upbringing, television and so on); and the other is by *deeds*, as through the experience of political freedoms by rehearsing and exercising them.

Interestingly, the system functionalist Talcott Parsons, impressed by the hippie and student movements of the 1960s and 1970s, predicted a further cultural revolution which would have its essential justification in the expansion and reform of education. Because more and more young people remain in the educational system longer and longer, Parsons argued that they undergo and experience an individualization in the sense that traditional commitments in life conduct are loosened or removed and the younger generation is subject to the natural compulsion of planning and putting together their biographies on their own initiative. In Parsons's view this is a cultural revolution in the sense that it brings in its wake a wave of loss of tradition in all fields of social action.

Thus one can distinguish two modes here in which the individualized code and norms of self-organization become an integral part of the self-design and self-consciousness of individuals. One aspect involves passing through educational processes and affirming norms of life conduct; these become the product of decisions that individuals must make, negotiate and justify. Parsons does not believe that this represents the threat of an atomization of society, or a collective utilitarian egoism, but rather, and this may seem astonishing, an emotionalization of social life. The other side of individualization is the search for meaning, a tangible meaning that can be actively lived out and is compatible with the forms of one's own life. The answer Parsons sees as emerging he reduces to the concept of 'love', which he understands in the broadest possible sense. One generation after another acts out the forms of religious and quasi-religious love, from self-sacrifice to the cult of the self.

Parsons is a thinker who understands and analyses the implementation of democratic rules in essence as *internalization*. There are good reasons to doubt whether such a thing as the spirit of freedom can ever really become at home in a society in this manner. Alongside internalization, the *experience of deeds* is the key experience that can not only make freedom an integral component of the self-image, but can also make the social reality of spaces of political freedom tangible to the individual. Anyone who demands and practises freedom soon learns that this always raises the question of power, so that the practice of freedom must experience and protect its own power bit by bit. Successes and failures may alternate or even be interwoven to the point of indistinguishability, but they both confirm the tight connection between freedom, power and autonomous action that characterizes the democratic spirit and the democratic self. In this sense, the everyday self-consciousness of freedom in a democracy does not arise from the teachings of books and schools, or from civil rights and constitutions (although these sources may be indispensable), but from active freedom which simultaneously, although perhaps only microscopically, shifts the power relationships of a society gradually into democratic reality.

Does that mean that the question of the spirit of democracy therefore turns into the question of how and where freedoms can be rehearsed and exercised in a society? If one starts from the distinction just drawn between biographical, inner-directed freedom and political, outer-directed freedom, then there are two areas where the struggle for freedom is being practised and experienced today. These are first, the turbulences of post-traditional life conduct and, second, the infiltration and assertion of demands for participation and self-organization in business and work, in churches and also in political parties, trade unions, parliaments and so forth. In traditional terms one would say that these are private and public places, but that distinction is applicable only to a limited extent. I suspect that there are multiple connections between sites of disputes and the experiences of disputes for biographical and political freedoms. To give a very mundane but also very powerful example, consider the fact that a single person's allotment of time and strength prevents a self-assertion in both sites, which makes it necessary to make biographical priorities, cuts and divisions of labour. On the other hand, as Alfred Hirschmann (1982) was aware, a kind of alternating disappointment may bring about a mobility of activity between the two sites. It is not the attraction of public acclaim, but accumulated annoyance with private frustration which drives people into political involvement and vice versa. What consequences and developments are connected and compatible with this is something that probably no one can foresee at this time.

On the end of the social ontology of cultural differences:
rights to freedom in diverse and uniform cultures

All these points of view converge towards an additional distinction, namely that between rights to freedom in cultures of *diversity* and rights to freedom in cultures of *uniformity*. According to Tocqueville, the age of equality is the age of uniformity. That is, the differences between people and cultures can be described, comprehended, justified and treated less and less as differences of nature or type. In other words, the differences between people are ontologically unlocked. From now on they must be asserted, staged, justified and renewed against the backdrop of uniformity in principle, that is, interchangeability. Uniformity implies, among other things, the end of the social ontology of cultural differences.

Taking this point of view as a basis, two stages of modernity can be distinguished in an ideal-typical sense. In the first modernity, the issue of who had access to rights to freedom, and to which ones, was largely answered and justified *ontologically*, by recourse, for instance, to gender, family affiliation, descent, ethnic 'blood ties' and the like, categories of social affiliation and identity that are distinguished by three features. First, they rely on the notion of separate worlds (between men and women, for instance), so that they assert clear definitions of inside and outside and the corresponding either-or rules of affiliation. Second, they apply with the authority and eternity of nature; they are therefore pre-ordained, closed to decision-making and require no further justification. Third, they fit (relatively) without contradiction, like Russian dolls, into a *national identity*; the separate realities of men and women are nested inside the family identity, the latter inside loyalty to an ethnic group, which in turn finds its crowning in the national identity.

In this first modernity of industrial society and the nation-state, the civil identity of the citizen (or *citoyen*) is completely tied into and dominated by particularistic loyalties of gender, family, ethnic group, class and so forth. The contradictions that exist in identity structure between universalistic claims and the particularistic reality of granted and denied rights to freedom are settled by and within the ontology of differences. Thus, for instance, with reference to their gender, motherhood and to the voluntary nature of marriage, central civil rights such as control of property, their own bodies, their own sexuality and so on were denied to women and transferred to their husbands until the beginning of the 1970s, even in Western countries. In the first modernity, then, the paradoxical nexus between inclusion and exclusion, inherent in the 'civil' rights to freedom from the very beginning, was ratified by and concealed by the cultural material of nature made available by the social ontology of difference.

By contrast, the panorama of a second modernity is now beginning to come into view, in which this ultimately essentialistically based architecture of unambiguous identity, with its clear definitions of inside and outside, no longer applies, because, in one way or another, the ontology of differences is worn out. Leaving aside the difficult question of why that should be (through cultural individualization and globalization processes, for example), we can run through the ambivalent consequences of this development. In, say, the relationship between the sexes, the conventional identities and roles of men and women which arose with industrial society are simultaneously shaken to their foundations, broken up and revitalized in modified form. This is expressed by men adopting and modifying elements of women's roles and women doing the same with men's roles, but clinging at the same time to the fragments of their natural identity, rebuilding it and staging it. Men perhaps become new-style fathers and yet remain more men than ever. Women struggle for professional recognition and simultaneously rediscover the maternal role as an alternative to a career, leading clever men to try to nail the old family order back together. In the struggle for the future of women beyond the female nature, *post*feminist and *re*feminist women's groups oppose each other at the same time as they flee to the front and to the rear. While some joyfully terminate the old female identity, others see the remnants and core of their female identity slipping away as the natural basis is lost, and they snuggle into the slogan 'equality without sameness' (Gerhardt 1990).

As far as the issue of 'ethnic identity' or 'racial' affiliation is concerned, in the wake of mobility in marriage and otherwise, divorce, remarriage and intercultural exchanges, this type of affiliation is beginning to be something that is no longer preordained and can no longer be read off from external features (such as skin colour). Instead, the 'race issue' or the 'ethnic issue' is becoming an option, which must be decided one way or the other. Who is 'black' and who is 'white', whether someone belongs to the large category of Hispanics, African-Americans or Asian-Americans (or all three) is a matter of agreed-on (thoroughly contradictory) rules. As empirical studies show, it is sometimes even a question that may be answered differently by one and the same person in different situations (in front of official personnel or inside the family).

In the second modernity, therefore, the identity structure of industrial society and the nation-state is losing its ontological cement, and hence its 'natural' definiteness. New identities, in the jungle of the global economy and in the struggle against the ecological self-endangerment of industrial society, for instance, are forming which no longer have their home in the cultural milieu of the nation-state. This starts with multinational conglomerates that push their employees back and forth on the international scene like chess figures. In the inevitable dealings with the electronic media, new figurations of intercultural labour forces arise; Robert B. Reich speaks of 'symbolic analysts' who work across cultural and national boundaries by intelligently using the Internet (1993: 129ff.). An oddly global sense of responsibility in response to the environmental issue is beginning to take shape, whose power is able to erupt with unexpected effect in global boycotts of (telegenically staged) 'spoilers of the environment' (Shell) or national governments (the French nuclear tests). In the struggle against a climatic catastrophe, new models of 'global management' are being designed and institutionalized at great expense and with great political consequences. Accordingly, the identity pattern of a *global manager* is gaining importance, amplifying the behavioural model of the national technocrat into a global ecocrat protecting international good conscience. On the other hand, something like an ecological citizenship is becoming significant for behaviour in a very everyday sense, from shopping to voting, all the way to issues of child-rearing in parental households, schools and the public sphere.

Associations such as Greenpeace and Amnesty International, Terre des Hommes and Médecins sans Frontières have become the object of hopes in recent years. Many view them as a new, third force between business enterprises and governments. This 'New Internationale' is present at all conferences and has by now constituted an effective, or at least a respected, corrective to the stagnation of international governmental politics.

The word is out that the contradictory unity of bourgeois and 'citoyen', as assumed in the scenario of the nation-state, is shattering. We are involved everywhere with a situation in which large parts of the bourgeoisie have long had to think and act in international categories, while the citoyen is still trapped in the national framework.

But a comparable transformation of the foundations, as one could summarize the discussion just sketched out, is also taking place in the relationship of culture and law. The legal form of political freedom, the juristic/political citoyen, one could say, continues to be tied into the laws and the normative system of the nation-state essentially without change, while the social form of perception of political freedom, the cultural citoyen, as it were, is fragmenting, losing and casting aside the ontologically clothed cultural clarities of the first modernity.

With this split between political and cultural citoyen, the contradictions already addressed and concealed in the coined word 'citizenship rights' are bursting forth openly. On the one hand, citizenship rights are world citizenship rights according to their universalistic claims; on the other hand, they are de facto national state citizens' rights everywhere, originally only rights for male bourgeois, not for workers, female citizens and others. In the transition to the second modernity, that is, with the end of the social ontology of cultural difference, various and antagonistic overlapped forms, mixtures and new identities are being formed everywhere, breaking open from the inside the pattern of preordained affiliations as collected and clearly delimited in nation-states. This also applies, as will be shown in the second step of my argument, to the authority relationships in the 'post-familial family' (Elisabeth Beck-Gernsheim 1994).

Youth as a form and avant-garde of one's own life

It is possible and necessary to demonstrate the contradictions between legal form and social form on the condition of women, that is, married women, mothers and so on, and this has often been done. Therefore a next step, the child's right to a 'life of his or her own', will be placed at the centre of attention here.

Many people who are committed to the rights of black people, refugees, the disabled and so on take it for granted that children 'belong' to their parents. Even if one gives a kind of secular blessing to this parent–child affiliation, it remains a fact that children are 'serfs' of their parents by virtue of their birth. Not much fantasy is necessary to imagine how later generations could rub their eyes in amazement at such a double standard. Slavery was abolished, but the private enslavement of children by their parents in the guise of care is coddled politically, legally and morally; worse yet, it is scarcely noticed.

Sweden is the exception:

> In Sweden, children are considered full citizens and simultaneously defenseless individuals who are just as much in need of protection in a certain way as are other minorities (Lapps, immigrants and so on) . . . Since 1973 there has been an ombudsman for children, who plays the role of an 'advocate' of children and has the task of sensitizing public opinion to the needs and rights of children and educating it about them. The ombudsman is not authorized to intervene in concrete cases, but he can exert pressure on authorities and political representatives, propose actions suited to improve the condition of children, remind adults of their responsibility for children and finally, provide children with advice and help through a telephone information service. It is evident that Swedish society concedes special rights to children (in the same sense as it once did to women, immigrants or any minority). There is a special institution that monitors the observance of these rights; the ultimate goal is the most harmonious possible integration of the child into society and the respect for his individuality. (Orfali 1993: 494)

In Western countries, children have by entitlement at least, not only their own space (see above) and their own (spending) money, but is also publicly challenged and supported as the subject of their own life. Thus for instance, the right of children to find out the name of their (biological) father is enforced in Swedish society with a certain degree of ruthlessness against any other reservations or taboos. The right of children to a life of their own is paramount. It is believed that the recollection of their own background is essential to their well-being.

In case the parents divorce, there is an analogous process. Children are granted the right to act on their own, in accordance with their age and their developmental status.

> This principle applies particularly in case of disputes after a divorce. The child must therefore have the status of a party in all proceedings that pertain to his guardianship and residency and visiting rights; moreover, he must be able to call upon legal representation. In the proceedings, he can decide through a court-appointed representative which of the parents he wishes to live with, even if his decision contradicts an amicable settlement of the parents . . . The child thus has the same claim to be heard and defended as any other citizen. (Orfali 1993: 494)

It is conspicuous that the state appears in the role of advocate of the child. The rights of the child to a self-determined life are even enforced against the parents if necessary. The protection of privacy is, to a certain extent, almost reversed here. In order to guarantee personality rights of the child, the state intervenes in the private sector, compels information and creates the 'transparent family'. Equality of rights for the child certainly collides with the protection of the family and requires or allows the deprivatization of private life to a certain extent. In other Western countries, particularly in the United States, there are similar trends.

Studies by sociologists of young people in recent years have shown that even without governmental intervention, without public transparency of the family, the model of a life of one's own has established itself almost automatically behind the walls of private life as a way of life for young people which is typical of the times. Against the background of a large empirical study called Youth '81, Werner Fuchs writes:

> Youth as a preparation for being an adult is being overlapped and interspersed by forms, or at least possibilities, of living on one's own responsibility and in one's own right. The phase of life that serves the formation of individuality increasingly contains places and challenges for activities that presuppose individualized. The age of life that serves

as preparation for individual life conduct is itself being individualized. The rite of passage is taking on traits of a biography of youth. (Fuchs 1983: 341)

This implies, first of all, that there are no longer any goals or certainties that must be 'drilled into' young people. Accordingly, the standards for the phase of youth are becoming imprecise and contradictory. Which is to say, conversely, that the objectives are being 'individualized', transferred back to young people's own design of the future. Since rules and standards of normality can no longer be conveyed and certainly not imposed on anyone, the personal backdrop of one's own life is projected on to the level of the social 'objective'. Public shrugging of shoulders and helplessness are transformed into the challenge to fill up the vacuum on one's own, on the small scale in personal life, and on the large scale in the life of society.

Unless the signs are deceiving us, this society can no longer be 'led morally and spiritually', because, and to the very extent that, it is individualized. With the propagation of a life of one's own as the normal way of life, the moral authority shifts back to individuals. The result is not the absolute absence of morality, but the design and justification of morality on the basis of and with the motivations of individuals, as well as the search for this new form of morality.

Second, young people no longer *become* individualized. They individualize *themselves*. The 'biographization' of youth means becoming active, struggling and designing one's own life.

A life of one's own is becoming an everyday problem for action, staging and self-re-presentation. It is wrested away with difficulty, fiercely defended and cleverly protected against any incursions from adults, who still don't know which end is up. This means that individualization itself becomes a topic and a conflict for young people. It becomes taken for granted, perhaps the core of one's self-image. Young people are avant-gardists of their own lives. They know how one must dig foundations for it, expand it and protect against meddling and collapse.

This diagnosis ultimately means that socialization is now possible only as self-socialization. A life cushioned from the inside against the outside has taken the place of paternal or maternal authority or that of governesses, teachers, policemen and politicians. Inner life is certainly still governed by social entities, such as the peer group, television, advertising and so on; just not the conventional functionalistic authorities and objectives.

The individualization of youth has a friendly, indifferent, consumption-oriented, hedonistic, aggressive, despairing and frightened face, but a violent one as well, for which violence for its own sake becomes the ultimate proof that something still exists and not mere nothingness.

That is how we are to understand the fact that 'the lifeworld of young people is visibly and inevitably [becoming] an arena of struggle for rivaling philosophies.' The 'uniform collective rite of passage of youth is decaying' (Olk 1985: 294). The different, often extremely disparate sources of meaning and experience for young people – school, television, advertising, the values and symbols of the chosen peer group, the strict performance standards of the world of work, the traffic jungle (their own car!), not to forget the well-meaning precepts of parents – all these force young people to conceive of and organize themselves as tinkerers with their own personalities.

'Youth' as a standard form no more exists than do young people with a fixed image of themselves. Identity is not to be pursued as a project that can be finished but becomes instead a *habit of searching*, which does not end and cannot and should not end. A life of one's own, particularly a young person's, is an experimental life, a probationary life. This includes identity, an 'empirical personality', permanently in need of self-assurance.

Anyone who concludes from this that being young today means living in a seething pot-pourri misses the central counterperspective: standardization. Young people, so argues Heinz Abels, are not inhibited about being normal. If one applies this to the prevailing confusion, this is even a preference for the deviant. If deviance becomes normal, the choice of normality becomes a precursor of protest. This is also based on an interest in ritualization that is awakened specifically in individualized society, which ultimately makes it possible to walk like Jesus over the waters of endless complexity. All of this presumes *self-normalization*, 'individual construction of a standard biography'. These individual constructions of normality dissolve the contradiction 'between the individual demand to be unmistakable and the vague feeling that the uniqueness is constructed from the "standard parts" of this modernity' (Abels 1993: 546).

To illustrate this, consider a scene from Milan Kundera: two young people caught up in the confusions of sexuality are unable to give in to their 'authentic' feelings. In the jumble of voices that they represent, they act as if in a film. The boy lives out a pornographic script that he once saw. He takes it off the shelf, so to speak, and plays it through. He sees himself in a double role: as a copy and as an actor in the copy he has chosen and is.

Young people act out rituals inside their groups. What is normal, how one acts, what one thinks, doubts or rejects, what is good, beautiful, worthless or right, 'in', that is determined inside the peer group (with props from television and consumer products) and rehearsed in a mutual conflict. The 'turf battles' between lifestyle groups which differentiate themselves and feud with one another on the basis of hairline distinctions in symbols and accessories, often nearly imperceptible from the outside, produce the external pressure for the internal rigidity and dogmatism that often appear to be characteristic of how young people divide and share the world. This also explains 'why young people at a certain age are deaf to any argument from outside' (Abels 1993: 546).

What consequences result from this for the *relationship of the generations* inside the family? Bernard Shaw once said: 'Old people are dangerous because the future is all the same to them.' One could vary this and turn it around to the effect that young people are dangerous because they *are* the future. To the extent that the future cannot be understood and mastered from the background, the power of youth grows. Given the fact that the future will be of a different nature, young people hold the strings for defining it in their hands. This is also and even especially true wherever the future appears congested by contradictions (for instance, the contradiction between the necessity for an ecological renewal of industrial society and the impossibility of achieving it). The idea that young people believe there is no future or that they are anxious about the future does not really question this view, it simply illuminates it from a different side. Because the future is contradictory, it escapes the grasp of adults and grows as a power, the power of young people to make decisions and definitions.

Patterns and vehicles of the generational conflict and compromise are typical of the times: arrangement and negotiation. Everything must be justified and agreed upon. 'Large-scale collisions between parents and young people have given way to a verbose, almost playful testing of limits in which the young people determine the pace.' Furthermore, Abels speaks of a 'dissociated understanding on lifestyles and life goals' as the compromise form in the 'collective bargaining' of the generations (Abels 1993: 546). In this way, both sides can keep face and go their own way. That is probably seeing and putting it too mildly, however. Mutual ignorance, at best tolerant indifference, appears to be a more apt description for the prevailing ceasefire between the would-be personalities.

Each side is leading its life with a free pass from the other side. Understanding is often just left out. Each side concedes the principles or reasons (or unreason) for decisions to the other side with equal parts of trust and mistrust. Tacit silence on the 'idiotic' aspects of the other is maintained across the trenches. Internally, on the other hand, there is whispering, puzzling and cursing over how deviantly normal the mind of the 'old folks' or the 'kids' really is.

The mutual concession of a 'space of one's own' or 'a life of one's own' corresponds to an *economy of conflict*. Letting the other side do what it wants is ultimately cheaper and more effective. In that way, the adults buy their own freedom and their own life. Anyone who grants their progeny the same can save the embarrassment – and futility! – of always claiming to have a better answer and other such authoritarian chest-thumping. No one has to take responsibility for setting a direction. This is how prosperity in the western part of postwar Germany makes possible an unstable conflict between generations based on *mutual ignorance of one another's real lives*.

In a very central sense, it is not quite possible (yet?) to speak of a 'democratization of the family'. The old authority structures may indeed be damaged, and certainly their paint is scuffed up. Negotiation is becoming the dominant pattern, as a demand. If the arguments and impressions presented here hold water, however, the elements of dialogue, of a virtual exchange of roles, of listening and taking responsibility for one another remain underdeveloped.

In 1995 the British research group Demos presented the results of a study of the sociology of youth which enquired particularly into the change in values between the generations. The authors, Helen Wilkinson and Geoff Mulgan, summarize their results as follows:

> This research has overwhelmingly confirmed the depth and extent of change; the rising power of women, the convergence of values between younger men and women, and the rejection of traditional restraints.
>
> But the research has also thrown up many surprises: the attachment to violence amongst younger women . . . the rejection of national identity, and the signs of a serious disconnection from society not only amongst groups like single parents, but also in a wider group of young people, both poor and relatively wealthy.
>
> But the core of the book is really about freedom. Most members of this generation take for granted that they can control their own lives, whether in terms of relationships or careers, lifestyles or beliefs. The old assumption that you had to inherit an occupation, a class identity, a religion and a standardized family life has gone for good. But with new freedoms come new problems: how to ensure greater commitments in family life; how to achieve stability in a far more fluid labour market; how to create a sense of common purpose and ownership in the political systems; and how to balance autonomy and interdependence. (Wilkinson and Mulgan 1995: 9–10)

For this generation, politics has become a dirty word. 'Over a third of 18–24 year olds take pride in being outside the system' (ibid.: 17). And yet the diagnosis of a 'me generation', a selfish generation, points in the wrong direction. What is negated is involvement in the established institutions, such as political parties, churches, trade unions, conventional organizations; more and more, these are being virtually avoided by young people. On the other hand, concrete personal initiatives for others, such as drug addicts, AIDS victims or homeless people is affirmed. A surprisingly large portion of young people are

> concerned about many issues: environment, AIDS, jobs and above all animals. Some analyse their disconnection in terms of contentment. But there are strong signs of discontent: deep-seated distrust of the system, and frustrated ambitions, particularly amongst women. Over half of under 25 year olds register as profoundly disconnected from the system, and a growing number of 'underdogs' are now prepared to bite back – we call them the 'underwolves'. (ibid.)

Understanding freedom as a social and political dynamic thus does not mean, and this should be emphasized, waiting for the downfall of everything good and beautiful in the midst of the vale of tears of a self-endangering modernity. Those who want (to activate) freedom, including its powers of social motivation and commitment and its creativity, must not close their eyes to narrow-mindedness, outbursts, episodes of intolerance, bloated philistinism, that is to say, very ordinary phenomena. Perhaps it is correct to accuse the theorists of grass-roots democracy and civil disobedience of glossing things over in this respect. Whoever would affirm the tradition of freedom as a social cement must also be prepared for outbursts of hate and violence. The ugly citizen certainly also creates new relationships in his or her own way. Of course, tolerance for that can and must be demanded, but that alone is not enough. Here, too, we will have think our way into, develop an insight for and practise the seemingly paradoxical logic, already discussed by de Tocqueville, of fighting the excesses of freedom with more freedom, specifically by means of experiences of freedom that awaken and renew responsibilities.

In sociology there is a peculiar grand coalition spanning all antagonisms and proclaiming in the most ringing tones of inner conviction that modernity needs, uses and uses up commitments, 'ligatures' (cf. Dahrendorf 1988: 17), just as the industrial system consumes natural resources. The diagnosis runs like this: modernity is counterproductive; it undermines its own (cultural, natural and other) prerequisites. This diagnosis, even if it has been proclaimed and elaborated by Martin Heidegger, Daniel Bell, Karl Marx, Max Weber, Arnold Gehlen, Ralf Dahrendorf, Jürgen

Habermas, Helmut Dubiel, and Ulrich Beck, is thoroughly false. This much is true, in any case: if the argumentation sketched out here becomes (or is made) tenable, then political freedoms represent an internal, autonomous, ancient and yet ultramodern source of meaning precisely for the second modernity, one which is not exhausted by daily use, but only flows stronger and more vigorously. Modernity, having placed freedom at centre-stage, is therefore not an age of disintegration, but an age of values in which the hierarchical certainty of differences is displaced by the creative uncertainty of freedom, including the dispute: what does freedom mean?

7

Misunderstanding Reflexivity: the Controversy on Reflexive Modernization

Starting points: institutional reflection (Giddens), reflexive community (Lash), unintended consequences (Beck)

It is hard not to misunderstand 'reflexivity'. In the book *Reflexive Modernization*, the concept and theory of reflexive modernization are understood and developed by the authors (without really noticing it) in two distinguishable and yet overlapping meanings (Beck et al. 1994). In the first view, represented by the chapters by Anthony Giddens and Scott Lash, 'reflexive' modernization is bound in essence (in keeping with the literal meaning of the words) to *knowledge* (reflection) on foundations, consequences and problems of modernization processes, while in the second one, represented by the present chapter, it is essentially tied to *unintended consequences* of modernization (thus deviating at first sight from the meaning of the words). In the former case, one could speak of *reflection* (in the narrower sense) on modernization, and in the latter of the *reflexivity* (in the broader sense) of modernization. In the broader sense, this is true because, alongside reflection (knowledge), reflexivity also includes *reflex* in the sense of the effect or preventive effect of *non-*knowing. Of course this terminology invites misunderstandings and is unfortunate in that sense.

A peculiarity and a difficulty of this distinction is that it is not really a sharp one. Thus talk of a century of unintended consequences cannot appeal to absolute, only to relative unawareness without contradicting itself, and the interesting issue is the type of this relativity: Who knows what, why and why not? How are knowledge and unawareness constructed, acknowledged, questioned, denied, asserted or ruled out? The concept of 'unintended consequences' ultimately does not contradict the understanding of knowledge in reflexive modernization; instead it opens an expanded and more complex game involving not just various forms and constructions of knowledge, but also of unawareness.

The approach to knowledge in reflexive modernization can be summarized, greatly oversimplified, as follows:

1   The more modern a society becomes, the more knowledge it creates about its foundations, structures, dynamics and conflicts.
2   The more knowledge it has available about itself and the more it applies this, the more emphatically a traditionally defined constellation of actions within structures is broken up and replaced by a knowledge-dependent, scientifically mediated global reconstruction and restructuring of social structures and institutions.
3   Knowledge forces decisions and opens up contexts for action. Individuals are released from structures, and they must redefine their context of action under conditions of constructed insecurity in forms and strategies of 'reflected' modernization.

A difficulty with this approach to knowledge is that some form of knowledge or other, consciousness, reflection, communication or self-observation, applies not only to all modern, but to all traditional societies as well. Indeed, as sociology has asserted in all its schools, from Max Weber through Georg Simmel to Erving Goffman and Harold Garfinkel, it is a fundamental characteristic of every social interaction. There is a beautiful image for reflection, this cognitive image that has been so central ever since the Enlightenment: vision with an eye inserted into it (Johann Gottlieb Fichte). This is the sense in which Alvin Gouldner speaks of 'reflexive sociology' and Jürgen Habermas of the 'communicative society'. In the talk of the 'self-referentiality of systems' (Niklas Luhmann), on the other hand, a quite different aspect of self-referentiality occupies the centre of attention. Measured according to the contrast between consciousness and unconsciousness, Pierre Bourdieu occupies a mediating position: he conceives of 'reflexivity' as systematic reflection of the unconscious preconditions (categories) of our knowledge.

The generality of the concept of reflection poses a problem for any epistemological theory of reflexive modernization. Either one clings to an undifferentiated concept of reflection, in which case the talk of 'reflexive modernity' becomes a mere pleonasm, or at best a grandiose tautology; or one distinguishes different modes and types of knowledge and connects statements on late or reflexively modern society to particular types of knowledge and reflection. This second path is the one taken by

Anthony Giddens and Scott Lash. This is the sense in which Giddens speaks of 'institutional reflexivity'. He means the circulation of scientific and expert knowledge on the foundations of social action. This licensed knowledge leads to 'disembedding' and 're-embedding', that is to say, it is employed for changing structures and forms of social action. Giddens conceives of both expert rationality and money as symbolic media of global, not just national, validity. This results in differentiations of space and time which ultimately open up the horizon of social lifeworlds to global systems and dynamics. The question arises: is 'modernity' therefore just a synonym for industrialism in Giddens's view?

It certainly is not. The provocative aspect of his theory of modernization lies precisely in the emerging antithesis of modernity and capitalism (industrialism). In contrast to traditional social orders, according to Giddens's basic thesis, modernity is characterized by a type of highly nervous 'institutional reflexivity' that is to be understood in a double sense. People do not simply react reflexively to systemic processes, they also adjust their social practices over and over again to changed information and circumstances. The 'institutional reflection' of modernity is the cause of its enormous capabilities, but also of the threat from the autonomy of its functional systems and the destabilization of its institutional foundations.

'Radicalized modernity' as seen by Giddens is the result of an 'autonomization of modern thought', which threatens to lose its powers to the extent that it pushes out beyond its boundaries. Corresponding to the 'globalization of modernity', as can be observed in the global interlinking of economic, political and cultural processes, are crises and conflicts on the institutional level, in which Giddens includes the capitalist mode of production, the industrial rearrangement of nature, and the forms of social surveillance. The more strongly the interaction between the institutional dimensions is dominated by the 'reflexive appropriation of knowledge', the more uncontrollable the global interconnections become within a world that is fusing increasingly together into a planetary unit.

In this way, Giddens simultaneously keeps his distance from postmodern doom and gloom. Modern society, he says, can neither be captured with Weber's image of the 'iron cage' nor characterized directly as the monstrous crisis into which Marx made it; instead, life in it resembles a journey on a 'jagganath cart', a metaphor with which Giddens refers to the old Hindu custom of travelling through the streets once a year with the image of the god of the same name in a gigantic cart (during which fanatic devotees of the religion occasionally threw themselves voluntarily under the wheels). The jagganath cart, according to Giddens, carries people over the abysses of time but crushes those who oppose it. For Giddens it is the symbol of an epoch that 'threatens to escape external control', but over which we still have a certain power.

Giddens clarifies the relationship of inherent systemic dynamism and human exertion of influence with the concept of 'trust'. While the relationships between people and their environment in traditional social orders were determined by standardized rules of behaviour and activity, which guaranteed something like 'ontological security', the members of modern societies have nothing left except the hope that the functional systems might fulfil expectations. Lurking at the bottom, however, is the knowledge of their instability and endangerment, which grows with the reflexive dynamization of modernity.

We are still living in an industrial society organized according to nation-states, to be sure, but we are already no longer living in it. 'Post-traditional trust', according to Giddens, is blind trust, a blank cheque issued to the functionality of abstract systems of knowledge and experts. This is how concrete, everyday actions are tied into a system of impenetrable global connections. A more or less successful mediation of 'anthropological certainty' in abstract systems in the corresponding socialization processes makes this 're-embedding' in global dependencies possible. The decisive point, according to Giddens, is the extent to which post-traditional trust can be converted to *active* trust. Active trust cannot be called up, but must be won. It should not be confused with duty, but instead requires substantiation. Ultimately, Giddens is concerned with the figure of the '*reflexive citizen*', for whom individual autonomy and responsibility must be readjusted to fit his vision and scope of activity. This figure also provides late modernity with a 'realistic utopia' which can give direction and impetus to a policy of reform. Of course, anyone who ties reflexive modernization to the dominance of expert knowledge, as does Giddens, misunderstands the pluralization of rationalities, and remains bound in a crucial respect to the conceptual world of a linear rationalization of knowledge (more on this point later).

Scott Lash also identifies reflexive modernization with modernization of *knowledge*, with questions of the distribution, circulation, consumption and enhancement of the substance and forms of knowledge, as well as the resulting conflicts. In his eyes, reflexive modernization is a modernization of knowledge, through which the foundations of social action and life (and thus the foundations of sociological thinking and research as well) become questionable, reorganizable and restructurable. More than Giddens, however, Lash sees new types of conflict coming about through different types of knowledge, which are simultaneously types of certainty. He distinguishes (connecting up with Kant) between *cognitive*, *moral* and *aesthetic* reflection. His attention focuses on the emotional particularities of '*aesthetic* reflection' which cannot be resolved emotionally, cognitively and morally and which create '*reflexive communities*'. Connected with this is the objection to Giddens and myself that our arguments are based on a cognitivistically foreshortened understanding of reflection (and thus of reflexive modernization). Against the background of advanced individualization and in the line of Anglo-American cultural theory and tendencies of 'new communitarianism', Lash considers the central issue to be 'reflexive communities'. These are understood in essence as a second and selectable naturalness of aesthetic symbolic worlds. These interconnect global markets, mobility, modes of consumption and local symbolisms and lifeworlds, and at the same time allow what had seemed to be out of the question: social, personal and global identities that are mobile, interchangeable, decidable as well as rigid, and suited to be lived out in a standardized manner.

Yet Scott Lash goes a step further (in collaboration with John Urry 1994); he also inquires into the new forms of social inequality which this society based on science, communication and information is generating as the dark side of its knowledge dependence. The distribution of information and opportunities for access to information networks do not just compel and enable the reorganization of production, circulation, capital accumulation and consumption by means of knowledge. At the same time, they present or, more accurately, construct, raised prerequisites of achievement and access that can lead to a radicalization of social inequality, all the way to the new fate of the 'outcasts', the 'dropouts' or the 'homeless', who slip through all the safety nets.

Thus Lash, unlike Giddens, poses the question of the *selectivity* of knowledge and *unawareness*, which is becoming central to future society as knowledge is modernized. He does not inquire, of course, into the role of unawareness in reflexive modernity, but rather into the possible new class formations in 'reflexive' society. For him this means science and expert society, but also information and communications society, subject to the tension between 'communicative rationality' (Habermas) and 'discursive power' (Foucault). That is, for Lash, 'reflexive' modernity is a modernity in which, on the basis of contentious cognitive, moral and aesthetic horizons of knowledge, consumption and identity, new rules of inside and outside, inclusion and exclusion are negotiated and established.[1]

The outstanding aspect of Scott Lash's contribution to *Reflexive Modernization* is how radically he poses the enquiry into the conditions that make community formation and commitment possible in contexts that Giddens calls 'post-traditional' and 'cosmopolitan' (and I call the second modernity). Here is where the controversy is situated for him, and probably for Giddens and me as well, and it is difficult initially to resist the spell of his arguments. 'Community', Lash writes, 'in whatever form, as "we", as a national identity or as some other collective identity, does not require any kind of hermeneutics of suspicion, but does need a "hermeneutics of recovery" which, in contrast to the masters of suspicion (and their present-day colleagues), is not constantly eliminating prerequisites, but makes the attempt to uncover the ontological bases for Being-in-the-World as a community' (Beck et al. 1994: 148ff.). Lash wishes to discover or uncover what predominantly holds people together under conditions of advanced individualization, now that this opposing factor is no longer a consensus on religion, status, class, male and female identities and the like.

In his extraordinarily well-informed search for an answer, he first eliminates everything that remains abstract and cognitivistic in the light of his concept of post-traditional community and everything that resists the pre-reflexively known everyday practice of Being-in-the-World with others. For him, all types of rational explanation, expert knowledge and interests miss this reality level of a commitment to the social which precedes any individualization. The categories of aesthetic modernity, such as allegory, mimesis and deconstruction, are equally unable to help.

For Lash this type of trans-individual counter-individualization forms within the horizon of *shared significance*, not in reflexive interpretation; in *active experience* and sympathy, not politically mediated experience; in *self-assured life praxis*, not political and ideological programmes of action, and so on. In a conceptually very subtle manner, Lash thus distils what is at stake for him: not to sacrifice the social too soon and uncritically to a universalized and internally contradictory theory of individualization that leaves its own prerequisites behind in the dark.

Lash, the constructivist of the first water, one of the outstanding thinkers in Anglo-American cultural theory, is thus attempting an 'anti-constructivistic constructivism'. His real opponent is not (only) the theory of individualization, but also those varieties of radical constructivism that decode collective identities as mere 'imaginary communities' and thereby (in Lash's opinion) ultimately tend to dissolve them. Taking recourse in Heidegger's 'workshop model' from *Being and Time*, Lash attempts to free himself from constructivism by turning it against itself, at least to the extent that a concept of 'reflexive community' becomes possible. This is equidistant from preordained traditions and from identities that are only socially constructed. It has its basis in (individualized) contexts of practical action in life, in which the *limits* of individualization are experienced and suffered, but likewise in outbursts of violence and recollected terror that inculcate cultural *differences* over and over again.

It is unfortunate that Lash does not also discuss Weber's concept of the '*political* community' in this context. This is based after all, similarly to the way Lash sees things, not in cognitive knowledge or the ferment of interests of social activity, but in suffered or inflicted *violence*, particularly, state and military violence (wars). In a political kind of 'concrete constructivism', this violence and the cultivated recollection of it continually create and inculcate, according to Weber, national and ethnic identities which are not grounded at all in anything original and natural (in fact, Weber argued vehemently against this). This supplementation is meant to show that I find Scott Lash's indefatigable and undaunted search for a simultaneously post-essentialist and post-constructivist foundation of individualized social action, as *produced* in the process of reflexive modernization, extremely important and stimulating, but am not really convinced of his results. It may simply be that Lash breaks off too early. Why is it not true that a number of different and contradictory social identities overlap in what Giddens and I call a 'reflexive biography'? But then how are we to understand the concept of 'collective identity'? What role do *political freedoms* play as a source of social commitments?[2]

Conversely, Lash's argumentation misses my point, namely the upsetting and transformation of the foundations of industrial modernization by its unintended consequences, understood as a conflict over unawareness, more specifically, the construction, circulation and destruction of knowledge and unawareness.

What distinguishes my concept of reflexive modernization from those of Giddens and Lash? To put it briefly and not too pointedly: *the 'medium' of reflexive modernization is not knowledge, but unawareness.* It is this aspect of the distribution and defence of unawareness that opens the horizon of inquiry for *non*linear theories (of reflexive modernization). We live in the age of unintended consequences, and it is this state of affairs that must be decoded and shaped methodologically and theoretically, in everyday life and politically.

How can the theory of reflexive modernization be understood and formulated as a theory of knowledge/unawareness? Stated in simplified form as theses:

1 The more modern a society becomes, the more unintended consequences it produces, and as these become known and acknowledged, they call the foundations of industrial modernization into question.

2 Unintended consequences are also part of knowledge. The only question is, who knows them and on what basis? Even the concept of '*latent* side-effect' does not mean *no* knowledge at all, but *one* knowledge whose claims are *controversial*. The talk of 'unintended consequences' thus denotes a conflict of knowledge, a conflict of rationality. The claims of different expert groups collide with one another, as well as with the claims of ordinary knowledge and of the knowledge of social movements. The latter may well have been developed by experts, but according to the hierarchy of social credibility, it is not considered to be expert knowledge and accordingly is not perceived and valued as such in the key institutions of law, business and politics. The knowledge of side-effects thus opens up a *battleground of pluralistic rationality claims*. This involves knowledge of the consequences of industrial modernization even on the lowest rungs of the ladder of social recognition.

3 This conflict does *not* run along clear and unambiguous associations of knowledge and unawareness, either in the sense of expert rationality or in the expert critique from activist movements. The characteristic is that, in the interplay of claims on *all* sides, knowledge and unawareness, limitations, selectivities, other relevances, rationalities, 'rationalizations' and dogmatism emerge (usually involuntarily), quite in the spirit of Karl Popper's 'critical rationalism' as expanded by the ruse of public reason. This conflict of rationalities implies that there is an enlarged (possibly difficult-to-delimit) horizon of competing agents, producers and interested parties for knowledge, in which the established linear associations of knowledge and unawareness become dubious.

4 As diffuse as this conflict is, it flares up over an objective. What is at stake is the defence or overcoming of institutional expert constructions of the inability of others (persons, groups, institutions, subsystems, countries, continents) to have knowledge regarding the 'side'-effects of organizational action. The question is: can the dams constructed around the unawareness of the foundation-endangering and foundation-changing consequences of industrial modernization be upheld, or will the recognition in its own centres of the consequences of knowledge-based industrial modernization change the basis of business, the social contract of industrial modernization, so that modernity becomes political? That is to say, the foundations and basic norms in business, science, politics and the family must be renegotiated and re-established.

5 In that sense, what is at stake in this conflict scenario (of a 'negative-sum game' of self-endangerment (Offe)) is essentially the 'preventive effect of unawareness' (Heinrich Popitz): prevailing constructions of unintended consequences, no matter what foundation in knowledge they are built on or questioned from, allow us to look the other way. They are constructions of (ir)relevance in an anticipatory defence against uncomfortable challenges (the moral and economic costs of liability or changes in politics and lifestyle) which intrude along with the recognition of the consequences and thus the responsibility for them.

Types of unawareness

In this sketch of an argumentation, the (terminologically unfortunate) distinction between reflection (knowledge) and reflexivity (unintended consequences) of industrial modernization is replaced by the distinction between knowledge and unawareness. However, this could simply mean replacing one unclear concept with an even larger one. The concept of 'unawareness' (as well as the overlap and possible potentiation of forms of knowledge and unawareness), after all, opens up new horizons of questions, but an unexplored jungle of meanings and misunderstandings as well. Unawareness can be known or not known, concrete or theoretical, unwillingness to know or inability to know, and so on. Of course it is out of the question to be able even to pose and elaborate all these questions of the analysis of unawareness in cognitive sociology in the context of a closing argument in a debate. Therefore, only a few aspects that play a part in the conflict of rationalities over 'unintended consequences' will be taken up here.

In his book, *But Is It True?*, Aaron Wildavsky demonstrated (on the basis of empirical studies) shortly before his death that the 'side-effect knowledge' of natural destruction and health risks which upsets the public also contains much unawareness – wilful omissions, mistakes, errors, exaggerations, dogmatisms:

> Looking back at the array of environmental and safety issues, many of which, like Love Canal and global warming, have become imprinted on the public consciousness, we can discern a clear pattern: the more that is known, the less reason there is to fear the worrisome object and the weaker the rationale for preventive measures. The one partial exception is CFCs leading to ozone depletion. (Wildavsky 1995: 24)

Wildavsky and his colleagues draw this conclusion from an analysis in which they compared scientific results and their presentation in public (television, newspapers) for a number of issues of 'environmentalism' or 'health risks'. The authors often demonstrate 'bad reporting practices' (limitation to *one* source of knowledge, for instance) or the mere allegation of the 'existence' of risks, which evidently are not considered to require any further substantiation. The exploration of risks, according to the authors, is obviously only a necessary but definitely not a sufficient condition for informing people about 'hazardous side-effects' of industrial activity. In addition there is the need to set up and practise appropriate ways of giving information and active ways of reacting to and processing this information on the part of the 'active citizen' (to put it in Giddens's terms).

In their informative question 'But is it true?', however, it is striking that even Wildavsky and his colleagues still proceed from a clear, unambiguous distinction between knowledge and unawareness. For them this is defined by expert rationality. They do not inquire into forms of (involuntary) self-discreditation of expert knowledge, for instance by risk diagnoses that change from one point in time, one institute, methodological approach and work context to the next. 'Unawareness' in the sense of distortions of expert knowledge by public media and 'translators' is therefore only *one* dimension of the key question 'But is it true?', but one which becomes central in the conflict of rationalities in reflexive modernization. The unwanted and involuntary revelation of half-knowledge, unawareness, repressed unawareness and the corresponding limitations in expert knowledge itself must be accepted (Beck 1992: ch. 7).

In general terms, at least the following aspects or dimensions of unawareness must be distinguished with regard to hazardous side-effects:

1 *Selective reception and transmission* of the knowledge of risk – 'falsification' in Wildavsky's sense (on all sides in public, of course, among social movements, but also among the various experts and organizations);
2 *Uncertainty* of knowledge (in a concrete and a theoretical sense);
3 *Mistakes and errors*;
4 *Inability* to know (which may in turn be known or repressed);
5 *Unwillingness* to know.

Wildavsky once again notes, very selectively: 'much of recent environmental and safety alarms are false, mostly false, or unproven' (1995: 42). This remark not only trivializes the 'knowledge' that has been worked out and is available on, for instance, the global effects of industrialization; more significantly, its seemingly clear distinction between knowledge and lack of knowledge conceals the central problem, the decision-making in uncertainty on all sides, which is becoming characteristic of the second, reflexive phase of modernity.

'Many of the essays in this volume', writes Albert Reiss in a chapter entitled 'The institutionalization of risk', 'are about how decision makers struggle with uncertainty, rather than risk, even when many risks (as in the case of the space shuttle) appear to be calculable. Decisions under conditions of both uncertainty and risk are, of course, subject to error. What is at stake is the acceptability of the error.'[3]

Wildavsky's central fear is that the rejection of error probabilities in the calculus of risk may lead to an overestimation of the hazards and thus ultimately to an overreaction and overregulation of all spheres of social activity in the sense of a preventive policy of risk avoidance. His demand is therefore: 'Reject the cautionary principle, reserve the environmentalist paradigm, stop regulating small causes with tiny effects!' That is certainly worth considering, but once again it very selectively follows the progressivistic idea that the greatest and most frequent errors are to be found, not in the realm of the experts, but among their critics, a unilateral attribution of errors and mistakes that conflicts, not just with the history of the sciences, but with the history of those particular controversies over the destruction of nature and threats to health with which Wildavsky is concerned.

Corresponding to the dogmatization of expert knowledge to which Wildavsky succumbs is a dogmatization of anti-expert knowledge to which many social movements succumb (with the 'good intention' of politicizing topics and circumstances). Uncertainties in one's own (risk) knowledge, it seems to many activists, interfere with political action: 'Effective management of highly publicized risks such as nuclear power and storing nuclear wastes, global warming and the greenhouse effect depends heavily on public trust in science, in technology and in managing institutions . . . Institutional legitimacy rests to a considerable extent on trust' (Short and Clarke 1992: 12). This indicates that, in the horizon of modernity, unawareness is viewed as a shortcoming or a failure.

Alfred Schütz and Thomas Luckmann distinguish various types of unawareness in their book *The Structures of the Lifeworld* (1973): 'The lifeworld is apprehended not only in that which it is, but also in that which it is not.' The elements of knowledge are structured according to 'cores of meaning, by degrees of familiarity, definiteness and credibility . . . Even without theoretical reflection, we know that we do not know everything.' The authors conceive of unawareness (in so far as it does not relate to the fundamental lack of clarity of the lifeworld) as *potential* knowledge. It consists of 'reconstructable knowledge', which was forgotten but can in principle be recalled, and 'achievable knowledge', of which it is known that one can learn it in certain ways (from a reference work or from education).[4]

In this conceptual frame of reference of an ultimately unbroken certainty of knowledge of the lifeworld, unawareness is predominantly conceived of as *not-yet* knowledge or *no-longer* knowledge, that is to say, *potential* knowledge. The problems of unawareness are understood from its antithesis, the knowledge, indeed the (unspoken) certainty, in which the lifeworld resides. By contrast to that, the *inability* to know is gaining in importance in reflexive modernization, as Anthony Giddens and Scott Lash stress. This is not the expression of selective standpoints, of momentary forgetting or of underdeveloped expertise, but precisely the product of highly developed expert rationality. Thus, for instance, the calculus of probability can never completely rule out a particular event. Or specialists in risk may question one another's detailed results, while other experts demystify the foundations of expert activity with their inborn thoroughness.

Against this background the question of deciding comes up again in a radical way. If we cannot (yet) know anything about the consequences of industrial research, activity and production (as is overwhelmingly the case today in the fields of genetic engineering and human genetics), if, that is, neither the optimism of the protagonists nor the pessimism of their critics is based on knowledge, then which rule applies? Is there a green light or a red light for large-scale utilization of technology in industry? Is the inability to know therefore a licence for action or grounds for *slowing down* action, for moratoria or perhaps not acting at all? How can maxims of acting and not being permitted to act be justified by the inability to know?

It is interesting in this sense that Wildavsky advises a kind of pragmatic scepticism in dealing with risks and information about risk: 'Nihilism is not the point. Distrusting everyone and everything, especially one's own judgment, is self-destructive. Instead, the citizen risk detective should learn to recognize patterns of misperception so as to avoid being controlled by them.'[5] In other terms, reflected doubt, 'effective distrust' (Wildavsky) definitely presents opportunities for a better public understanding in dealing with the (in many respects) 'uncertain' knowledge of risk.

Linear and non-linear theories of knowledge

One can and must therefore distinguish between *linear* and *non*-linear theories of knowledge of 'reflexive' modernization, with the ability to locate this distinction essentially in the question as to the distribution and defence of unawareness. This distinction cannot be mapped unambiguously on to the authors of *Reflexive Modernization*: it runs across them.

(1)   Linear theories imply (usually tacitly as the converse of their central assumption) that unawareness is *not* relevant (central) to reflexive modernization. Non-linear theories assert the opposite: types, constructs, and consequence of unawareness of risks are *the* key problem in the transition to a second, reflexive modernity.

(2)   While linear theories of knowledge assume (more or less) *closed* circles of formally responsible expert groups and people who act on knowledge, non-linear theories see an open, *multiple* field of competitors acting on knowledge. In the limiting case, two scenarios confront one

another here: the expert monopoly or the *technocratic* decision model on the one hand and, on the other, the late modern 'palaver' model, in which it is unclear who is *not* allowed to participate in the discussion. In the zone where the two models overlap, this problem arises: how can rules of admission and procedure be agreed on and practised with consensus and dissent simultaneously?[6]

(3) Linearity means knowledge based on the *consensus of experts*, limited numbers of recognized and licensed practitioners inside research institutes and organizations and the corresponding explicit, cooperatively interlinked sites for producing, acknowledging and implementing knowledge. Non-linearity means *dissent* and conflicts over rationality, and hence principles, that is to say, unclear, uncooperative and oppositely polarized networks of people and coalitions acting on knowledge (Hajer 1995). They play out conflicts with antagonistic strategies and complementary chances for success in subsidiary public spheres over (in the limiting case) *contradictory certainties* (images of nature and humankind).

(4) The distinction between and distribution of knowledge and unawareness is thus based on a social structure, a power gradient between individuals, groups, authorities, monopolies and resources (institutes, research funding, etc.), on one side, and, on the other, those who call them into question. This distinction, turned concrete and sociological, is the correlative of a rationalization conflict which is very difficult to delimit. The talk of 'unintended consequences' signals a stage in the conflict in which homogeneous expert groups are *still* capable of excluding other forms of knowledge and the people using it as unawareness. To the extent that they can no longer manage this, linear modernization ends and non-linear modernization ('reflexive' in *my* sense) begins.

(5) The criterion for this is therefore closed versus open; consensual versus dissenting networks of agents, questions, methods, governing hypotheses, scenarios, assessments and evaluations of risk and danger. Why is this distinction so central? Because the issues of unawareness (in the double meaning of *inability* and *unwillingness* to know) erupt there for everybody; moreover, that very state of affairs brings about a compulsion to open oneself to 'outside knowledge', the outsider perspective. This is how the foundations of the oblivious monorationality (economic, technical, political, scientific and so on) characteristic of linear modernization are shattered; this same monorationality is being exaggerated even today in the form of systems theory (with the insinuation that functionality and autonomy depend precisely on screening out the outsider perspective).

Both factors – the inquiry into our *own* inability to know and the ability to empathize with outside rationalities – mark the transition to the second modernity of (self)-uncertainty which is both constructed by civilization and known. Only then does the question gradually come up of how these antagonisms and differences in *known unawareness* can be related to one another, worked out and joined into procedures for reaching decisions in new forms and forums.

Both approaches to reflexive modernization, knowledge and unintended consequences, have a number of points in common:

- They are opposed to theories of postmodernism, for instance;
- They emphasize the key significance of knowledge for the reorganization of modern societies;
- They explicitly see that reflexive modernization must not be confused with *Enlightened* modernization and certainly not with *self-controlled* modernization; on the contrary, both viewpoints agree in emphasizing the central importance of constructed uncertainty, that is, self-generated risks and dangers, in modernity as it becomes inwardly and outwardly globalized;
- They also do not see the motor of reflexive modernization in something new, but rather in the familiar crisis-wracked production cycle of capital, technology, labour, science and the state.

Unawareness, unintended consequences and self-endangerment

Yet the following distinctions (beyond what has already been said) are worthy of noting and discussing.

(1) If one demonstrates 'reflexive modernization' (as I do) not on the distribution of knowledge, but on the distribution of unawareness of side-effects, then one cannot ascribe the adjective 'reflexive' either to traditional societies or to classical industrial modernity. This concept of 'reflexivity' is, after all, formulated much more narrowly than the difficult-to-delimit concept of 'reflection'. It only seems paradoxical that known, repressed, maintained and attacked or recognized and admitted *un*awareness marks the separation line from 'reflexive' modernization.

(2) The approach to knowledge in reflexive modernization (as represented by Giddens and Lash in different variants) seems at first sight to be supported by the fundamental cognitive-sociological insight of modern constructivistic epistemologies that all phenomena are constructed in

knowledge, while the side-effects approach seems to become entangled in the contradiction between 'seen and unseen'. In fact, the concept of 'unintended consequence' only raises the programme of cognitive sociology to a more complex level. The distribution and circulation of knowledge is simultaneously undermined, parried and supplemented by the distribution and circulation of unawareness. As mentioned above, this opens the way to reflexive modernization's non-linear (negative) theories of knowledge, the possibilities of which cannot be exhausted here. The introduction of unawareness as the key conflict in 'reflexive' modernization forces distinctions.

(a) So far everyone has always spoken of the opening of the knowledge agenda by conflicts over *selective inference*, which attempts to move up the ladder of credibility from unawareness to knowledge.

(b) *Reflected unawareness*, however, must be distinguished from this. This follows the pattern that one knows that one does not know and what one does not know. Thus knowledge and unawareness are separated within knowledge.

(c) This brings about regions and zones of known inability to know. The issue of how knowledge of the *inability* to know is to be evaluated, whether it means, for instance, a green light or a red light for technological development, is highly contentious in the insecurities of self-imperilling modernity.

(d) On the other hand, repressed or *unknown unawareness* ultimately means ignorance. One is unaware of what one does not know. This is found among experts and counterexperts, as well as in the hysterias of new (and old) religious and social movements.

(3)   The cognitive image of the unintended consequence does of course reveal a certain combination of knowledge and unawareness. It is generally known (independently of the gradations of knowledge and unawareness in the concrete case) that unseen, screened-out 'unintended consequences' do not erase the self-imperilment they signify, they intensify it. This is related, among other things, to the fact that 'unintended consequences' presuppose *actions*, and thus subjects, practices and institutions as well. The latter do not stop functioning because of the unawareness of the unintended consequences, but are in fact favoured by it. Knowledge of unintended consequences has an inhibiting effect on presumed routines of action, and this becomes unnecessary as the unintended consequences become better known. The theoretical knowledge of unintended consequences thus also contains, in this cognitive image, the implication of the paradoxical *intensification* effect of unintended consequences *because* they are not known. This effect is very closely

tied to definite (more or less verifiable) items of knowledge (hypotheses), such as the assumption of causal relationships contained in the metaphor of the 'dying forest'. The prerequisite is that there be knowledge of un-intended consequences (the 'dying forests' in this case) and that this know-ledge be acknowledged. Then the active desire not to know does not halt the death of forests and the extinction of species, it *accelerates* them by not stopping or correcting the dynamics of industrial self-endangerment.

(4) 'Unintended consequences' are thus a paradoxical (negative) cognit-ive image, in which (under certain circumstances) unawareness is *known* as an intensification of self-endangerment, presuming that there is a believed knowledge of the consequences, whatever its basis in specific cases. The power of social movements and a public inspired by science to make alternative definitions is based on this fact: the more emphatic-ally the believed knowledge of industrial self-endangerment is negated, the more threatening the 'actual' potential for endangerment becomes (behind the facades of unwillingness to know). The knowledge contained in the knowledge of industrial side-effects allows, or perhaps forces, a distinction to be made between *known* and *actual* ('objective') endan-germent. In pointed terms, it rests on the cognitive construction of an *in-itself*, an 'objective' active world of constructed dangers of civiliza-tion independent of our knowledge or unawareness of them. In fact, it even contains a built-in hypothesis of amplification and exacerbation (independent of knowledge of the concrete case). Active unawareness – ignoring and hushing things up, that is – *intensifies* the 'actual' dynamic of the routine self-endangerment in industrial modernity, which is prac-tised independently of our knowledge of it. In that sense, the inquiry into the types of unawareness enlarges the narrow, linear perspective of cognitive sociology by the immanent distinction between the known and unknown, but thereby intensified dynamism of action of industrial self-endangerment.

(5) This social construction of a knowledge-independent and thus 'objective' endangerment, however, is not true in and of itself. Instead, it needs focused investigations and the appropriate indicators. The ques-tion arises of the *social construction* (and sociological reconstruction) of 'objective' indicators of hazard and destruction. My answer is based on two considerations: the 'objective' indication of self-endangerment is tied back into the mutual criticism of social agents. The presumption is that, wherever established expert rationalities come into contradiction, there are indicators of an *institutionally constructivistic* 'objectivity' of the hazard indicators.

The central example of this, in my view, is the *principle of private insurance*. It proclaims that private insurance enterprises man the border-crossing between the risks of industrial society (still considered socially controllable) and the self-constructed threats of risk society (*no longer* considered controllable, because they render even the institutionalized bases of calculation and control inoperative). With their verdicts (based on economic rationality) of 'uninsured' or (more radically) 'uninsurable' (why is irrelevant), the insurers contradict the engineers, scientists and industrial executives who appeal to technical calculations of risk as they brush aside any reservations of a concerned public with gestures of inno-cence, and attribute (virtually) *zero* or vestigial risk to uninsured and uninsurable forms of production, products and technologies.

'Vestigial risk' means: 'we don't know, we can't know.' This inability to know is of course not really ever expressed, but generally distorted into a certainty. 'Vestigial risk' is the language of repressed uncertainty within the horizon of putative (cognitive) certainty – no more than high-flown claims to perfection and control. The words 'vestigial risk' *negate* the knowledge of unawareness. But it refers to it and announces it. The knowledge of not knowing (or being able to know) is, one could say, relegated to the irrelevance of a footnote.

(6)   Thus I come back to the 'politicization of modernity' (see chap-ter 1 of the German translation of Beck et al. 1994): this erosion of the foundations of technical, scientific and industrial action politicizes modernity, not only within the officially labelled political system, but also in business, in organizations, even in private life. In this sense, con-gestion has become a metaphor for the involuntary politicization of modernity. It symbolizes the forced utopia of self-limitation. Congestion means the involuntary sit-down strike of everyone against everyone else, technically imposed mass Buddhism, an egalitarian forced meditation for drivers of all classes of cars. 'You're not caught in the congestion, you are the congestion' is written in large letters in a tunnel. Thus con-gestion becomes the quality of an entire culture. This does not mean just traffic congestion, but the infarction of modernization in general. The linear modernity of 'bigger, faster, more' is at risk of infarction every-where. This applies, as we have found out by now, to the ecological infarction, but also the infarction of the welfare state, wage labour society, the transportation system, the pension system and so on. The implac-able 'more' and 'faster' of primary modernity collides everywhere with the problems, erosion and obstructions it generates: destroyed nature, empty coffers, more demands and fewer jobs despite, or perhaps because of, the economic upswing and economic growth. This is how politics becomes

unbound, while the established political institutions are left behind as ossified and partially non-functional masks of themselves.

Summary: points in dispute

What then are the points in dispute? More than anyone else, Anthony Giddens confronts the question of what is being broken up with the question of what is being created. He uncovers the dependencies of global expert systems, emphasizes the role of 'institutional reflexivity' and inquires into the possibilities of 'active trust', which cannot simply be called upon, but must be created and won. That is how he describes in progressively clearer strokes the 'reflexive citizen', who must master and define politically and biographically the emerging uncertainties of the detraditionalized order on a cosmopolitan scale.

Yet, in equating reflexive and *expert-determined* modernization, Giddens underestimates the *pluralization* of rationalities and agents of knowledge and the key role of known and repressed types of *un*awareness, which constitute and establish the discontinuity of 'reflexive' modernization in the first place. Giddens thus misunderstands the questioning of the foundations of expert-determined modernization as well as the various efforts to create forms and forums of debate inside and outside of organizations in order at least to tie these contradictory rationality claims into a discursive context and a consensus on procedure.

Even where this does not happen, the question is: how does one deal with the competing rationality claims, that is, with the creatures of unawareness that are flourishing in the shade of a self-endangering modernity? To repress or to acknowledge (on *all* sides), that is the Hamlet question which is being posed on the dividing line to the second, non-linear modernity.

In contrast, a double construction of unawareness characterizes linear modernization. First, *other* forms of knowledge are blocked out and rejected, and second, we deny our own *inability* to know. This does not apply just to experts, but to activist movements as well. The former stand with their backs to the future and operate in the false self-assurance that comes from having denied their unawareness. The latter dogmatize their (un)awareness for purposes of political intervention. It is precisely this admitted uncertainty which opens up the context of action for industrial modernity. Both groups would have to look at themselves from the outside, so to speak, in order to understand and shape reflexive modernity's horizon of uncertainty in constructive political terms.

Both issues of the second modernity – the deliberate acknowledgement of outside perspectives and rationalities on the one hand, and the explicit working out and processing of unawareness on the other – do not really become an issue for Giddens.

We must agree with Scott Lash that aesthetic reflexivity is also a key issue of reflexive modernization, and one which I have woefully neglected. His inquiry into the conditions and possibilities of 'reflexive community formation' is equally deserving of attention and urgent action. This inquiry is, after all, situated at the intersection of debates in social philosophy, ethics, sociology and politics regarding the bases for cohesion in self-endangering modernity. But what is his answer?

If I have understood Lash correctly, his response is tantamount to a type of 'unreflected originality'. Following up on Heidegger, Lash attempts to make this simultaneity of background, staging and reason plausible and transparent by hermeneutic means. What comes to light in the process (or what I have been able to understand of it) is not free, no matter how liberal its intentions might be, to *re*-ontologize what has just been *de*-ontologized in reflexive modernity, namely cultural difference. In any case it is impossible to rule out the danger that the re-lived transcendence of ingrained, emotionally charged and aestheticized ethnic, gender-specific or national identities may ultimately fall prey to very banal reifications and may thus duplicate concrete political constructions of cultural difference. Scott Lash must face the question as to how he distinguishes between communities that are 'reflexive', in his sense, and those which are *countermodern*.[7]

To pick out only one example to stand for many: particularly in the United States, it is more and more common (and thoroughly reflexive) for self-representation to be the only form asserted and accepted as legitimate for representing a group.[8] Any representation by others (for instance, the representation of blacks by whites, women by men or gays by straights) is considered to be 'racist' and 'sexist' by definition. It is easy to understand how this negation of the universalistic exchange of viewpoints and perspectives comes about, namely as a defence against repression and as a reaction to pluralization and individualization. It is completely obvious to me that Scott Lash does *not* mean this type of, one could almost say, 'postmodern racism'. But what remains to be clarified is how this can be spelled out in the context of his highly interesting inquiry into the intramodern sources of commitment in individualized lifeworlds.

The crucial issue of reflexive modernization, however, is this: how do 'we' (experts, social movements, ordinary people, politicians, not to forget sociologists) deal with our unawareness (or inability to know)? All of us, not only the authors of *Reflexive Modernization*, are far from answering this question.

8

The Renaissance of Politics in Reflexive Modernity: Politicians Must Make a Response

I

A farewell letter from Joseph Stalin has been found in the archives of the Kremlin. In it there is the statement: 'Comrades, rest assured! If – contrary to expectations – communism, not capitalism, should shatter from its own contradictions, then dissolve the Soviet Union, unite Germany and see to it that Moscow enters NATO. The West will never recover from the blow.' To be sure, this is apocryphal but laughing at it leaves behind a bitter taste, because it is actually being performed in the real-life cabaret of history. Montesquieu once noted that 'institutions perish from their success.' Gradually the dialectic irony is dawning on us that the West disappeared along with the East.

There is no longer a Federal Republic of Germany. We are living in a phantom republic. Just as someone continues trying to use an arm even after it has been lost, we talk and act in the phantom language and the phantom world of a West that no longer exists. There is no longer a European security system, no policy of equilibrium and deterrence, no first and third worlds (simply because there is no longer a second world), and there is also no NATO and no West Germany any more.

There are only fictions of the same name, structures consisting of questions, a gigantic political vacuum laboriously covered over and tenuously held together beneath the glossy paint of victory. How it will be filled up is the central conflict in Europe, beyond any recession or defence crisis.

This vacuum is covered by a false consciousness. Many people hide away, make themselves comfortable and mutter the rosaries of post-modernism (end of politics, end of history, pointless, too late) while all around them politics erupts again from the rubble of the East-West order.

The renaissance of politics arises from two overlapping movements. With the collapse of the East, the foundations of Western politics have crumbled into a heap of rubble despite the brilliance of the triumph. This in turn is the prerequisite for the ability, in almost all fields of politics, to reinvent the coordinate system and to reset and realign the switches. Both phenomena, the shattering of the old foundations and the reformulation, even the re-formation of politics, are still taking place in Germany (unlike Italy) behind a facade of stability and continuity.

The implosion of the East has made possible something like a 'gutting of politics' in the West. The Biedermeier facades of the old Western republic are maintained and cleaned up, while inside not a single brick or principle remains in its accustomed place. The conservative language policy-makers have coined the false magic phrase 'new normalization'. In the guise of adaptation, this amounts to practicing a backward somersault. This makes it possible to turn back the clocks of modernity in Germany almost without any legitimation.

The East–West antagonism was one gigantic cementing of politics. The roles were fixed and the antagonisms extended into everything. On both the small and the large scale, the zones of normality and deviation, neutrality and partnership were staked out and planned all the way down to the details of industrial production, municipal politics, family policy, technology policy, military and foreign policy. From Uganda to Eritrea, from Helsinki to Bonn, in Paris, Moscow, Warsaw and among the imprisoned leaders of black African liberation movements, everyone knew what to do and what not to do. The force-field of this global mega-antagonism absorbed the freedom of action in foreign and domestic policy. This just barely permitted something as bold as the German *Ostpolitik* of the seventies. But even that was constantly required to defend itself against the suspicion of intending to East-Germanize West Germany.

The conflict mechanism of the East–West antagonism thus abolished politics in the strict sense of the word. The thesis of the 'end of politics', as worked out and elaborated in Western thinking, is the thesis of the end of politics within the East–West antagonism. Where everything, the roles and opposing roles, the moves and countermoves, was in principle written down as in a great script and constantly mutually affirmed in general activities, there was a 'politics of philological interpretation' on this or that twist and turn in this or that situation, but nothing like politics in the autonomous, creative sense of the word. The collapse of the Eastern bloc turned this script into scrap paper. It continues to exist only in people's heads.

An epoch that is convinced of the futility of any action gets caught in the maelstrom of political revolutions and challenges that confront political fantasy as never before – and give it opportunities. There is an involuntary renaissance of politics from the rubble of the old world order. Assuming this diagnosis hits a nerve of the emerging future, then politics (or political science) should be a centre of interest. An age which, for the best of reasons, has bid adieu to action skids back into the political sphere, and fundamentally this time. A modernity that is fatalistic at least in its mind is transformed into a political modernity, in which constants are shifted, rebuilt and exchanged. From the reorganization of the familial and gender order to the ecological reorganization of industrial society to the reorganization of Europe, everything is in flux, at least for one historical moment. Indifference, which had joined and allied with hopelessness, is revealed as an ideology of the old West because these good old arguments, which still govern people's minds, misunderstand the freeing of politics in the collapse of the old order.

One can attempt to capture the galloping pace of history in two interpretations. First, the old East–West antagonism has been replaced by a West expanded by the East, a Greater West. Everything is as before, only more, larger, with fewer alternatives and less criticism – the end of social history (which need not mean the end of wars, revolts and so on). Second, a West without an East no longer is a West. A West which is joined by its Eastern counterpart loses in the glory of its superiority the very thing which had made it the West: the external antithesis that made it possible to restrain and glue together internal rivalries and particular interests.

In positive terms, this means that Europe is not a reality but a possibility, a factor X of which only one thing is certain: it is not a known quantity or a constant, but an unknown, a variable that only takes form while it is being designed.

In order to understand what is happening in Europe today, one must keep an eye on what *could* happen if the necessary institutions, which need to be invented, already existed. These include European parties, a European public sphere, a European foreign policy, a European security policy, the expansion of NATO eastwards and so on. Everywhere, only the political forces and institutions that exist are in action and not those which must be founded. This negates two things: first, the explanation of events from the way things currently are, and second, the explanation of events from the past. The anticipation of something new becomes an integral part of an explanation of what is happening before our eyes and could and would happen differently if this factor X to be invented actually did exist. In other words, a healthy amount of realistic fantasy is needed to track down a reality which has become conceptually mobile.

'The most urgent dangers to the security of Germany loom in the East,' writes Robert B. Zoellick:

> Will the reformers prevail in Russia? Will Russia accept the independence of Ukraine in the long run? Will the Ukrainians be willing and able to create a stable security structure without nuclear weapons? Will unrest in Eurasia send waves of refugees to the West? Will poorly designed nuclear power plants or other ecological disasters poison all of Europe? (1993: 10)

A 'new *Ostpolitik*' is needed, to include or attach the post-socialist societies, including Russia, economically and in domestic and foreign policy to the European Union and European policy. Eastern Europe was once the bread-basket of Western Europe, but because of the division of Europe the West Europeans developed an agriculture of their own, which today blocks the importation of agricultural products from Eastern Europe. Only a new economic division of labour can smooth the way to Europe for Poland, Hungary and others. If Europe does not manage the economic inclusion of the former Eastern bloc, the new democracies east of the German boundaries will scarcely be able to survive.

'It almost takes away one's courage even to approach thinking about these issues. Germany's West European partners seem so overcome by the scope of these problems that they are practically paralysed. Unlike them, however, Germany can afford neither national self-absorption nor short-sighted entrapment in an inward-looking West European discussion' (Zoellick 1993: 10).

Has this society, has Europe become politically shapeable? That is certainly the case. The first to recognize this were the conservatives in all parties and on all levels of society.

II

The apt question, 'What's left?' (Steven Lukes), which is dividing left-wing groups and splinter groups, has been discussed to death. It is high time to turn the tables and ask 'What's right?' Is the right really right? An inquiry into the contradictions of conservatism must be put on the agenda!

It is not just the idea structure of communism and socialism or the prime example of the Swedish welfare state which are falling apart; the theories of the social free market and the nation-state are too; in fact the entire conceptual world of neonationalism is like a blind person describing colours when dealing with the situation that has arisen in world civilization. If there is indeed a glut of anything, then it is the windfall of contradictions from the right-wing tree of knowledge. Here we shall pick out only one particularly rotten apple: the remarkable incompetence of nationalism.

Thinking within the context of the nation-state has lost any capacity to act on the problems that are moving the world, from environmental protection to global economic interconnections and migration to issues of regional and global peacekeeping. This can be demonstrated, ironically, in the German attempt to close its own borders in an act of national sovereignty to ward off the flood of refugees (the so-called 'Drittstaaten-Regelung'). That required a dam of friendly adjacent states. Everything giving impetus to nationalism in Europe, mass unemployment, streams of refugees, wars, is ironically international.

Capitalism, socially and democratically tamed, and now suddenly being sanctified, also has a flaw woven into it which will limit its ability to expand. It remains dependent on the destruction of the environment. In that sense, this economic form is a social order for a privileged minority of the world's population. The more clearly the destructive consequences of the free market reach popular awareness, the more obvious the privileged position becomes, with a double effect. The great majority of the world's population must be denied a similar way of life and the prosperous fortresses of the West are then invaded. In other words, ecological destruction generates social inequality and poverty on a global scale. Poverty can no longer be conceptualized in national terms; it must be understood as international and mobile poverty, with completely new challenges to institutions, politics and science.

Some time ago, Joachim Fest regretted in an editorial that the 'ultimate taboo' of the former West Germany, the 'moral verdict on the Hitler years', is now going up in flames. But was it only the throwers of fire bombs who broke this taboo and not the writers of fire bombs as well? Did Dr Helmut Kohl, the political symbolist and historian, not also break this taboo quite consciously on 20 July, the day commemorating German resistance to Nazi barbarism, when he met Ernst Jünger, the antithesis of this resistance? How was this violation of a taboo among the people and the elite of Germany possible? More pointedly: how do citizens get together to become a bogeyman for their own class?

In Germany and in other countries of Western Europe, a rebellion is raging against the eighties, a '*Kulturkampf*' between two modernities. The integrity of a highly individualized society is to be replaced, using the contrast to 'foreigners', by a society that is unequal internally and built up like a fortress externally. The goals are Adenauerization, back to the future of the fifties, yodelling high-tech.

To put it ironically, since men can no longer withhold the vote from women, since it would be difficult indeed to reduce women's desire to get educated, since everything that would be useful in trying to hold them back just doesn't look right, the not quite conscious and not quite unconscious result is a detour to achieve the same in the dramatization of force and the national. This provides an explanation for the violation of the taboo against right-wing radical violence that has so far not been widely recognized: the counterrevolt that has built up even in the West against the individualization, feminization and ecologization of ordinary life.

Like their Islamic counterparts, the fifties fundamentalists in all parties and at all levels pursue their cause indirectly. In the former case, people pray to the Koran and use Mohammad to restore domestic tranquillity, while in this country people float on the neo-Nazi wave. All it takes is a little controlled excuse-making for right-wing violence, and the political coordinates already begin to drift rightwards. With carefully measured containment and exclusion, the government can sharpen its 'liberal image'. This is how one gets others to do the dirty work and then slips into the role of saviour of democracy against the excesses. When will the political catch-22 into which the conservatives have manoeuvred themselves, morally, psychologically and physically, finally be recognized and made use of?

Conservatism is just as bankrupt as communism. Political ideologies and systems are tottering on their foundations everywhere. The reason is the increasingly obvious and utter lack of any basis of legitimation. This is how great state systems can be brought down by civil disobedience, as has already happened in Italy.

The accusation against the conservatives in all governments and parties is not that they are actually pursuing only one interest, their own. A society in which the people in power were simply as self-interested as you or me would be happy indeed. To be consistent, a society which gets outraged over that would have to dismiss itself. The accusation is lack of imagination, dilettantism, continuing in the same rut, tying oneself down, exhaustion – and only then, corruption.

III

The former general secretary of the Christian Democratic Union, Heiner Geissler, has warned his party against the folly of nationalistic *Realpolitik*. An exporting nation like Germany, which literally lives from the free

exchange of goods and ideas, is destroying the basis of its own existence by excluding 'foreigners'. Does 'Germany for the Germans' mean
that, from now on, American, Japanese, Israeli and Arabian capital
will be subject to the asylum-seeker laws and blocked by neighbouring
states for investment there? The more stridently conservatism strikes
neonationalistic chords, the more severely it will endanger its own economic power base and competence. Neonationalism produces unemployment. *This* endangerment of the 'German business climate' (the so-called
'Wirtschaftsstandort Deutschland') is scarcely mentioned.

The unifying commitment to anticommunism concealed the contrary
tendencies that are linked together in the conservative camp, and these
are now moving apart. There are values conservatives who take the word
'preserve' seriously and therefore contradict the market conservatives,
who count on stimulating a qualitatively unchanged economic growth,
thus further heating up the primary industrial machinery of dissolution
and destruction. They, in turn, are in conflict with the statist conservatives, who pound on the nationalistic and military keyboard to combat
the malaise that the other conservatives produce.

Interestingly enough, it was Friedrich Engels who noted and denounced
this contradiction between capitalist planning and military build-up.
Of course, he drew the conclusion, bloodily refuted in two world wars,
that capitalism is 'in essence non-militaristic' (Schumpeter). The contradiction between dead investments in the military and the cosmopolitan
interests of capital in globally open markets and borders is frozen in the
classical national consciousness, but it can be activated at any time,
particularly in view of empty public coffers.

Military and foreign policy attempt to contain these tendencies. It
must be recalled that the old tablets of law have also shattered in this
field of politics in order to recognize how casually facts of a nationalistic
German global policy are being continuously created. Quite incidentally,
political responsibility for governmental policy has apparently shifted
from the Chancellory, Ministry of Defence and the Ministry of Foreign
Affairs to the generals. How else is one to explain why the strategy paper
by General Inspector Günther Naumann, in which the 'legitimate interests' of Germany are postulated and propagated in a global context, was
elevated shortly thereafter as the guiding principle? One reads in the
Naumann paper that 'A view concentrating exclusively on Germany or
Europe will not do justice to the security of Germany and future challenges', and then the Minister's 'defence policy directives' to implement it
declare that the 'new normalcy' includes, among other things, the 'main-
tenance of free global trade and unfettered access to raw materials and
markets around the world in the context of a just world economic

order'. Where 'politics as a profession' (Max Weber) fails, profession as political action has an opportunity. This is a classic case of rule-altering military and foreign policy *from below*, foreign and military subpolicy by the military on its own initiative and for its own benefit. This recourse to linguistic formulas dug up from the imperialistic nineteenth century is neither a coincidence nor an accident, because this world-view is likewise intended to be renormalized by the establishment of a General Staff.

Once upon a time, there was a country which took it for granted that in a democracy the primacy of politics over the military was to be maintained under all circumstances and in all questions. Like other taboos, this one was violated, not observed, by the governing pseudo-conservatives.

On the whole, the decline and rise of national conservative politics can be studied in exemplary fashion in the demise of the old 'domestic Bundeswehr' and its re-establishment as a 'global Bundeswehr'. Just like NATO, the old Bundeswehr was built on national defence. Its equipment and doctrine, its power, its prestige and its legitimacy thus stood – and fell! – with the one reliably dangerous aggressor, 'communism'.

Because the new Germany is 'encircled by friends', as Defence Minister Rühe puts it so refreshingly, 200,000 soldiers were given their victor's laurels and their discharge papers in a single stroke. If defence policy had remained defence policy, the domestic Bundeswehr would have become a kind of western East Germany, a self-liquidating army in which everything shrinks: jobs, money, prestige and public tolerance of manoeuvres.

How deeply the fear of being without enemies has affected the military is evident from how far they went to point out their usefulness. The generals suddenly discovered a concern for the starving people of the world, for environmental protection, disarmament, and the struggle against drug trafficking and international arms smuggling as an expansion and ornamentation of their peacekeeping military calling – necessity is the mother of invention.

In a country which, for the first time in its strife-filled history, finds itself 'encircled by friends', it is noteworthy what a flourishing trade there is in all possible and impossible enemy stereotypes, with the eager participation of intellectuals of all persuasions. The trend ranges from the interchangeable enemy (Islamic fundamentalism, Iraq) to the mobile enemy (the arms trade, nuclear proliferation) to the abstract enemy (asylum seekers, foreigners, a global civil war). Finally, any momentary enemies gap can always be closed by fundamental reconsideration, for instance by presenting the enmity as insuperable. This anthropological flexibilization of enemy stereotypes makes it possible to have enemy stereotypes without enemies. The more irrevocable and impenetrable the threats, the larger and more varied will be the future markets for security producers, peacemakers and military technologies around the world.

Those who link together the two concepts 'national' and 'global' in the assertion of 'global German' interests are committing a dangerous category error by confusing and commingling the nineteenth and the twentieth centuries. Illusory recognition is blocking off and replacing cognition almost everywhere. Here this 'deceptive déjà vu' (Jürgen Habermas) becomes history making.

'The conception of modern military interventionism', writes the military historian Wolfram Wette, 'reveals the following elements':

1 An 'all-round alarmism', interpreting the international situation as a vast field of actual and potential dangers;
2 The political will to define international 'responsibility' and national interests exclusively in the terms of power and military policy;
3 The re-legitimation of war as a means of politics;
4 The resumption of the striving for a German 'world power role', which constituted the central foreign-policy orientation of the German power elites from the founding of the [second] Reich until 1945. Today this is normally a purified striving, seeking to avoid earlier errors as much as possible: no going it alone nationally and only a limited acceptance of risks. (Wette 1993: 5)

Though appetite often develops in the eating. It is a truism that institutions must not be judged by the intentions of their founders, but must be designed such that even their successors and the successors of the successors cannot break ranks from the fundamental democratic, civilian consensus. This brings up a question that is oddly hushed up: what would *institutionally* hinder military power posturing by later German governments towards neighbouring states aimed, for instance, at revoking the renunciation of the 'eastern German territories'?

The construction of a global Bundeswehr presumes the dismantling of thought and action in nation-state categories and national interests. A step across our own borders with weapons in hand can be responsibly taken only by sacrificing national sovereignty rights in, as the conservative political theorist Hermann Lübbe says, 'large-scale political institutions *sui generis*'. These are not to be conceived of either as a federal state or a confederation of states, but rather as 'equipped with partial sovereignties for performing functions which the individual states have de facto long since lost the sovereignty to perform. This extends from the economy through environmental protection all the way to defence policy' (Lübbe 1994: 33).

IV

Thus we reach the core of the question: why is there this glorification of the national in a transnational world?

The national is certainly not, as is once again being 'proven', a sub-terranean circulatory system of history that was forgotten and repressed and is now erupting violently and bleeding once again. 'Nationalism is by no means the awakening of nations,' writes the historian Ernst Gellner. 'People invent nations where they had previously not existed' (1964: 169). The national is an (original) invention of the nineteenth century, a left-wing weapon, moreover, against the prevailing dynasties appealing to God.

'Popular sovereignty' was asserted and aroused against these dynasties, cutting the bond between the other world and the monarchy and re-establishing this-worldly governance. This was pure heresy, for which for centuries people were sentenced to burn at the stake. It also was and is necessary for the diversity of 'natural' unity to be suppressed in order to open and protect the national space governmentally and culturally.

The Chinese have a curse which they address to their worst enemies: 'May you live in exciting times!' The renaissance of the national is a toxic antidote to this curse of a decaying world. The same goes for all the key concepts of the ongoing conservative counterreformation: nature, woman, man, people, ethnic identity and so on. These categories invoke ancient and anthropological things, things that are unchanging and must simply be accepted. They invoke the rebirth of simplicity after its demise. Countermodernity absorbs, demonizes and sweeps off the table the questions that modernity brings up, puts on the table and reinvigorates. People say 'nature' but they practise 'naturalization'.

The propagandists of countermodernity live in contradiction, how-ever. They can never redeem what they promise. With one hand they accelerate the autonomous course of modernity, and with the other they constrict social freedoms. It is the masquerade of the past, performed as an actual drama on the stages of modernity. The attraction on the pro-gramme is the re-enchantment of the national after its demise.

The demonstration that an inherent connection exists between Marxian theory and the inhumanity of Stalinism must be followed (immediately) by the demonstration of the affinity between any kind of nationalism and the atrocity of 'ethnic cleansing', this barbaric slaughter in the heart of Europe. In the opposition between communism and nationalism we are dealing with the pleasant alternative of 'hanging or strangling'. So far the attractiveness of strangling arises from the fact that hanging has lost its appeal.

Someone who wishes to strangle himself and other people ought to say so openly, but no longer derive a justification from public denunciations of hanging.

V

What conclusions result from this for a public-oriented social and political science? The constellation for criticism in Germany has never been so favourable. The petrifaction of criticism which the predominance of Marxian theory implied for a century is gone. Big Brother is dead. Now one can take cognizance of the highs and lows of his prevalence again and with astonishment. Only for petrified thinking is this collapse tantamount to the end of criticism. In fact, criticism is now finally able to catch its breath and open and sharpen its eyes.

Post-Marxian social criticism, or let us put it more clearly, *antisocialist criticism* of society, can begin only after the collapse of the East–West antagonism. The constraints on thought, perfected in Stalinism to the point of self-torture and self-destruction (and vividly depicted in Arthur Koestler's novel *Darkness at Noon*), but which also kept the Western left captive in a 'double bind' between socialistic critique of capitalism and socialistic critique of socialism, are only now becoming inapplicable.

Where then is one to find and apply the lever of criticism today? Is there not a fundamentalism of instrumental rationality in all Enlightenment which is always easily able to convert Enlightenment into its antithesis? Perhaps, however, this very critique of primary Enlightenment is the prerequisite for the beginning of an *alternative* Enlightenment, one which is not afraid of scepticism, but makes it the very element of its life, indeed its survival.

Perhaps a way of life of humane moderation will result from deliberately chosen, admitted and accepted scepticism. Perhaps error, constantly pointed out, is the only way to bring us to our senses. Perhaps reflected scepticism, living and arguing on the level of the times, will overcome industrialism's arrogant faith in technology and will justify tolerance and curiosity for others? *Dubito, ergo sum*: I doubt, therefore I am! I doubt, therefore I become! I doubt, therefore I give you space! You doubt, therefore you acknowledge me! You and I doubt, therefore we are! We doubt, therefore we become possible! We doubt, therefore there are multiple modernities and we start everything all over again.

Scepticism, contrary to a widespread error, makes everything possible again: ethics, morality, knowledge, faith, society and criticism, but differently, a few sizes smaller, more tentative, more revisable and more capable of learning and thus more curious, more open to the unsuspected and incommensurate, with a tolerance based on and rooted in the ultimate final certainty of error. After Marx, Engels and Lenin, after Horkheimer and Adorno, perhaps Montaigne ought to be rediscovered as the founding father of the social theory of the new reflexive modernity.

Perhaps the political programme of radicalized modernity is scepticism? Established doubt, after all, requires a different distribution of power, a different architecture of institutions, a different technology and technological development, a different science, different groups in which to learn, and decisions that can be revised.

9

The Open City: Architecture in Reflexive Modernity

'Cities make people': urban planning and urban policy, like law and the study of human genetics, are forms of applied social design (Schütz 1992: 35). Architecture is politics with bricks and mortar, even though architects may envision only aesthetic goals. The city must be reinvented in a world that threatens to choke ecologically, in which the economy is pulled into the whirlpool of 'systemic rationalizations', as production and work are reorganized and redistributed across the boundaries of departments, firms, sectors and consumers. This is a world in which the traditional nuclear family is an 'endangered species' in need of protection, where people seek new forms of exchange between 'personal life' or a 'personal space' and the forms of the social they make possible; where identities become unclear, selectable, multidimensional and contradictory and where fear generates new (electronic) walls. But how is that possible?

I would like to distinguish two forms of the city in the future and the models of architecture related to them, namely the city of Either-Or and the city of And. This distinction goes back to an impetus from Vassily Kandinsky. In an essay with the title 'And', he raised the hybrid question of whether there might not be a keyword that characterizes the nineteenth century and our own, respectively. His answer was that the nineteenth century served Either-Or, while the twentieth century had embarked on a search for And. For Kandinsky this meant, in essence, synthesis between, for instance, art and technology. Yet the horizons opened up by the words 'Either-Or' or 'And' go far beyond this. Separation, delimitation and restriction, the desire for clarity, manageability, security and control characterize the former, while the latter is marked by diversity, interminable globality, the issue of the context, cohesion, experiments with the included middle, the affirmation of ambivalence, and irony. The question of the city of And is the question of the city in a world grown interminable.

The urban Either-Or began early in Judeo-Christian culture as the separation of religious inwardness and worldliness, morality and indifference, (religious) affiliation and (potential) hostility. The principles behind the segregation change over the centuries: estates, professions, ethnic affiliation or industrial classes – city planning as containment of the 'worker peril', a dam against communism and finally the functionally structured city which, when fully developed, became the 'Taylorist city'. Still, the talk of functions from city planners has strongly metaphorical traits. There is no recognized system of functions; crude divisions, such as work, residence, technical infrastructure or social infrastructure are 'far removed from the real city' (Hofmann-Axhelm 1993). The context, the And, could never be ruled out. It became a topic (in good capitalist manner) at least as a path, exchange and trade/transit route.

Post-Taylorist industry is currently discovering the productivity of the 'pigsty coefficient', that is, the irreducible subjectivity and chaos of the work process, as a source of creative solutions. Similarly, the functional dividers and delimiters encounter the productivity of mixed spaces and intermediate spaces, the productivity of And. What does location mean for (social) identity? How does the designing of spaces and intermediate spaces become the creation of public spaces, the formation of social structures?

A life of one's own – a space of one's own; this is the formula that has fundamentally shaped our postwar architecture. In the struggle for a 'space of one's own' there is more at stake than just the spatial structuring of everyday life. What is at stake is withdrawal, self-control and subversion, shaking off external and internal compulsions. The democratization of space in the sixties, which many smirked at then and sharply criticize today, is a good bit of everyday emancipation turned into architecture. The unpredictability of social life begins here and in this way.

The general development can be displayed by the example of Munich. The population *declined* over a 20-year period (1972: 1,338,924; 1987: 1,253,282; 1992: 1,320,643) while the number of residences *increased* (1972: 509,437; 1987: 626,688; 1992: 660,736). The much lamented 'housing crisis' in Munich, with its drastically increased rents and land prices, thus does not result from a smaller number of residences (or residences which are too small), but from an increased demand for housing and higher standards, as well as better material prerequisites to satisfy these. The contrast of *fewer* residents, *more* residences and a *growing housing crisis* expresses the power with which the struggle for a space of one's own changes everything: architecture, urban planning, the housing market, land prices, transportation systems and so on.

A space of one's own does not create a social identity, however, not even a personal one. Even for private consciousness, identity springs from the intermediate spaces so woefully neglected by architecture, the public domain, the neighbourhood. And this question of the identity of social life becomes increasingly important as individualization advances. Even the distinction between good housing in bad neighbourhoods and bad housing in good neighbourhoods makes this clear. The latter is desired and the former is avoided.

It is possible to speak of a serial polygamy of urban neighbourhoods. The rich ones get married over and over again to the poor ones in order to consume the essence of specialness, the social ecology of the neighbourhood.

'Our most recent projects are mostly public buildings and articulations of the collective,' says Rem Koolhaas,

> and this at a time which really resists that and no longer has any programmes to articulate that which is public . . . There is Derrida, saying that things can no longer be whole; there is Baudrillard saying that things can no longer be authentic; and there is Virilio saying that things can no longer be real. I feel that architecture has the duty to oppose these tendencies.

The point is 'to reformulate the thought of a "communal institution" in the midst of the complete collapse of public space – against the obvious homogenization of the electronic media, against the loss of place, against the triumph of fragmentation' (Koolhaas 1993: 24).

Behind the initiatives for reviving the deserted central cities is the struggle for the city of And. This is directed against the extinction of functionally separated spaces in the rhythm of the times, but also against interventions of control by the community from above and below and against the regimen of exclusive difference. The search is for a culture and architecture of *hospitable spaces* (Schütz 1992: 47). This makes things possible that seem mutually exclusive: intimacy and anonymity, communal spirit and freedom. Everyone is able to come and go, to be an extra or a featured actor on the stages of semblance (café, boulevard). 'Smooth, ice-cold, elegant but not soigné, somehow always slightly, ever so slightly reminiscent of a hairdresser. Disastrous if this type gets involved with intellectual things' (Tucholsky 1985: 145).

A strategy dominant in Germany today, however, ultimately comes down to retraditionalization or, more acutely, renationalization. The national Either-Or is intended here to foster community and identity.

The central example for this is the petrified vacuum of Berlin after the East–West conflict. This is now supposed to be filled up and national-istically glamorized with the fictions of capital city architecture. Here the idea of a city, more precisely a capital city, as the site of identity formation literally becomes concrete. The meaning of the new Germany some day is being anticipated architectonically, as it were. The need of a frightened political elite to protect itself from 'annoyance with politics' is also mixed in here. The anti-urban feelings of the provincial political princes in Bonn are working themselves out in designs for pompously overdressed 'government districts', well shielded and yet accessible almost without contact. A mild taste of this is provided by that mausoleum to Franz Josef Strauss in Munich, the new Bavarian state chancellory, a hybrid of a bureaucratic Winter Garden, a hothouse for paperwork and a palace à la Ceausescu. But where is the revival of the Berlin that lives in the paintings of Kirchner or Grosz, the city whose incorruptible insol-ence inspired Gottfried Benn?

However one may imagine the new modernity, it will be characterized by an increased quantity, perhaps even a different quality, of insecurity, as variation, diversity, dissent or conflict, but also by threats and dangers that escape the typical standards for calculation. In the familiar view, this means *angst*, with all the expected consequences, including political ones. The contrast of 'safe–unsafe' threatens to determine structures. Mike Davis invokes the spectre of an 'urban ecology of fear':

> The system of video monitoring by cameras with which the pacified zones of the central city are observed has been extended to parking lots, pedestrian areas, squares and so on. This dense ring of observation opens and constitutes a virtual omnipresence, a space of protected safety. White-collar workers, administrative employees and well-heeled tourists congreg-ate only in these identified spaces, only here do they feel safe, settle down and spend their money. Video-monitored office and store entries combined with private security systems, panic buttons available everywhere and emergency telephones protect the daily routine. (Davis 1992: 23)

The exclusion of drop-outs into new 'hyperghettos' represents a dramatic intensification of the Either-Or. Such areas arise as a defence against threats to life, as a bastion against criminals, using all the tools of the police and electronics, and in that sense they no longer recognize the exchange of functionally separated spaces. The Either-Or is radicalized into a *Neither-Nor*.

At the forefront of the movement of civilization looms a highly modern *architecture of apartheid*, not based primarily on racist prejudices, but rather on the needs for security of the 'productive elites' (as they are called so charmingly in our country). There are no longer any (overt) exploitative relationships with the poor and the poorest, as Marx claims, but simple needs for distance from the brutalization and barbarization of capitalist civilization in its most advanced stage. In this climate of Neither-Nor, things which should be kept separate are mixed up: the *insecurity* arising from the break-up of traditional forms, lifestyles and certainties of life and the *threat* from indiscriminate violence and criminality.

These are completely different challenges that require different types of answers. A social policy of Neither-Nor gains the power to establish itself not least by deliberately dramatizing both the decline of values and the threat of criminality.

The American social philosopher Michael Walzer has suggested a distinction between 'single-minded space' and 'open-minded space'. The latter signifies meeting places of the excluded which take away the fear of things that threaten under the rules of chance and freedom by exciting curiosity and mutual interest. Promenading on boulevards or frequenting cafés, which the early moderns praised so exuberantly, provide just a first taste of this.

The threats that call the very substance of the metropolis into question speak two languages: that of criminality *and* that of the environmental crisis. In this respect, the calm before the storm is also present in architecture. It is less a matter of existence (transportation, for instance) and more one of design (shopping streets, for instance). If it is true that the city represents the laboratory of civilization, then it is decided here whether and how the Either-Or of urbanity and ecology can be preserved in a new synthesis of both.

The politics of Either-Or alleges: either modernity and thus self-destruction, or stopping, going back, asceticism and then, possibly, salvation. The politics of And counters: modernity *and* ecology. The question of an ecologically sensitive lifestyle is answered here with the search for a *highly* urban lifestyle. It is necessary to invent and create spaces for living, working, being together and confronting one another that can satisfy the needs and desires for more, further and faster experience and enjoyment of the variety and contradictions of the place. That is certainly easier said than done. The decline of the world on the one hand and dutifully sorting out rubbish for recycling on the other only make sense to people of 'good conscience'.

Hong Kong is often cited as a bogeyman in opposition to this demand for more modernity and enhanced urbanity to cut down ecological self-destructiveness. That is a misunderstanding, however. In this case, as so commonly, status quo modernity is confused with *alternative* modernity. The attempts of Richard Rogers to create an ecological Manhattan of integrated functionality in Shanghai point more in the direction of an ecologically radicalized modernity.

In the antithesis of the two architectures of the future, therefore, the issue is not an intelligent utilization of technologies and resources, but rather the discovery or invention of an *alternative* modernity. The slogan 'back to the future', which helps itself to the costume chest of the past, is opposed by the creative further development of modernity, the struggle to redefine social life in a simultaneously globalized and individualized world. Anyone who understands architecture as politics turning into stone must point out all the forks in the road that open up here. If one wishes to sharpen the alternatives, one can say that the point is to counteract the tendencies of exclusion and nationalistic pomp by enabling or renewing urban democracy. Modern Germany arose from the fundamental decision against the two totalitarianisms, fascism and communism, which tortured and destroyed this century. This requires an architectonic expression. In my eyes, this is the search for a city (or an architecture) of the experimental And.

But how do we build the city of And? What challenges arise along with it for architects and planners, for politicians, for citizens? These requirements are clearly different from the key words and values that have been the basis of debate so far; they operate *beyond modernity and postmodernity*. A reflexive architecture of And is not indifferent to where it builds. It inquires into the particularities of spaces and the public and identity-creating power of the intermediate spaces. Postmodernity, the self-infatuated play with styles and errors of architecture, has become too postmodern for it. It wants more. It is not indifferent to ethical-political issues of space. On the contrary, it searches for communitarian ways of founding a 'city of individuals', for an architecture which, with the attentiveness that was needed to elaborate private space, now also inquires into creating public spaces, 'open-minded spaces' whose spontaneity must not be confused with the buildings of the organized public sphere, with schools, museums and city halls.

Isn't this a fundamental overtaxing of architecture? I don't think so. This is not a confusion of architecture and politics. But architects are not fools concerned only with structures and trends, and even less so in the phase of reflexive modernization. Architecture as a school of aesthetics is one side and its sensitivity to the social ecology of place to be developed is the other. The reflexive architecture of And discovers the history of the place and expands it into the public sphere. It says: 'Even if I cannot change society, I would at least like to influence the way people pass through the spaces, the way they perceive their connection and cohesion in the spaces, including the built-in contradictions.' For me, the broken up features of Berlin have something of this perforated charm of unprotected hardness and inconsistency which, in Kracauer's phrase, lets 'the real conditions show through'. 'Without art, nothing works any more,' says Joseph Beuys. I should like to add, 'Without the art of And, nothing works anymore.'

When Zarathustra, 'passing slowly through many peoples and through numerous towns', went 'slowly back to his mountains and his cave', writes Nietzsche,

> he also came unexpectedly to the gate to the great city; but here a foaming fool jumped toward him with outspread hands and barred his way . . . 'Oh Zarathustra . . . here great thoughts are boiled alive and cooked till they are small. Here all great feelings decay: only the smallest rattlebone feelings may rattle here . . . Don't you see the soul hanging like a limp, dirty rag? And they still make newspapers out of these rags!'

Finally Zarathustra interrupts the foaming fool: 'I despise your despising; and if you warned me, why did you not warn yourself? Out of love and love alone shall my warning bird fly up, not out of the swamp' (Nietzsche 1954: 287–9).

Who are the 'foaming fools' today? Probably those for whom critique of the city and pessimism about it do not stem from the magic of the city. The great city is lived-out utopia and experienced destruction of this utopia all in one. Or, to put it in a variation of a phrase from Basho: living in Munich, I long for Munich.

10

How Neighbours Become Jews: the Political Construction of the Stranger in the Age of Reflexive Modernity

It was Zygmunt Bauman and Shmuel Noah Eisenstadt who called attention to the meaning of the site of the conference on Modernity and Barbarism. A plaque in front of the conference building states:

> Square of the Jewish Deportees
> In 1993, 24,000 Jews lived in Hamburg. From this point, thousands of Jewish citizens of Hamburg began a journey which ended in the death camps of the Nazi regime.

The difficulty of the choice of words 'Jewish citizens of Hamburg' points to the problem I wish to discuss: it was not 'racial Jews' (*Rassejuden* according to the Nuremberg Laws) but (Jewish) neighbours who, through publicly stirred up hate and bureaucratic measures, were made into strangers, into alien-blooded, 'racial Jews', who were to be 'cut out of the body of the German people' (in the undisguised wording of the 'Laws for the protection of German blood').

In her book *Aus Nachbarn wurden Juden* (Neighbours became Jews), Hazel Rosenstrauch writes:

> When power was handed over to Hitler and the NSDAP [National Socialists], the life of the Jewish minority was determined far more by adaptation to their environment than by the common bonds that had developed

from hundreds of years of persecution. A multiplicity of philosophical, religious and regionally based differences were concealed behind the term 'Jew' ... There were religious Jews and Jews who, at best, went to the synagogue during the high holy days and who understood of Judaism about as much as their Christian neighbours understood of Christianity. Among the believers, there were followers of reformed Judaism and orthodox Judaism, each with their own synagogues, rabbis, and schools ... Communists and socialists from Jewish homes, whose self-understanding and way of living no longer had anything do with Judaism, also became 'racial Jews', as did baptized Christians, who sometimes first learned about their Jewish grandparents when they had to produce verification of their Aryan heritage. There were committed Jewish socialists, conservatives, and even a small group of German nationalist Jews who identified themselves with the ethnic concept of Germanness. (Rosenstrauch 1988: 11ff.)

The Association of Jewish Combat Veterans, Jewish socialists, German nationalist Jews, Eastern Jews, exotic even to assimilated German Jews: all the differences, oppositions and contradictions between them had to

be deliberately disregarded before 'the Jew' could become the most successful symbol of Nazi propaganda ...

The magic formula included everything which was in opposition, everything which did not fit into the simple, clearly depicted and defined Nazi conception of the world. Trade unionists, critical intellectuals or artists who could not be stamped as 'Jewish' on the basis of 'racial science' were derided as 'lackeys of Jews', or 'Jewish degenerates' or as 'contaminated by Jewish Bolshevism'.

German society, after all, formed a 'national unity' only very artificially, for a short time and formally. The 'standard Jew' is a variation of the longing for national unity. The 'German *Volksgemeinschaft*' emerged only from hatred against everything unfamiliar, against the complexity of a democratic society with all its conflicts. (Rosenstrauch 1988: 16ff.)

This aspect can be generalized in a certain sense: we speak today not only in the sense of a civic, but also of a cultural identity of gypsies, Turks, asylum-seekers, and also of Germans, French, Swedes, Russians, etc., as though something substantial and singular were indicated that is possible to define and distinguish. An essentialist difficulty is inherent (particularly in German language) in these and other nouns, which consume and silence indistinctiveness and ambivalence, in other words, the socially and politically constructed character of cultural identities.

How neighbours *became* Jews is well documented.[1]

It was not just some 'gangs' or criminal associations – as some memorial stones at the sites of former synagogues today suggest – who had been destroying Jewish businesses and organizations even before the so-called 'Kristallnacht'. Out of concern for the prestige of the thousand-year Reich and to provide 'calm in the economy', the chancellory of the Reich regularly had to intervene when the assaults took on a life of their own beyond the scope of the planned disturbances . . . First there was an increasingly refined definition of that which was 'foreign to the German character', an 'enemy of the state' and 'non-German', and then, after the German population and countries abroad had been prepared, the National Socialists renounced considerations that complicated the image of the enemy. (Rosenstrauch 1988: 31)

How neighbours *become* Jews in the present and future, or more generally, how neighbours become strangers and enemies, is the topic of this article. I wish to discuss this question in four steps:

1 What does the category of *'stranger'* (Fremde) mean from a sociological point of view?
2 How can the transition between simple and *reflexive* modernity be understood?
3 How does the *social construction of strangers change in reflexive modernity*?
4 How do stereotypes of the stranger become *enemy stereotypes*?

I

What does the category of the 'stranger' mean? We will begin with a few examples. Strangers are not Prussians in Prussia, but Prussians in Bavaria (or, conversely, people originally from Munich in Berlin). Strangers are not Turks in Turkey, but rather Turks in Berlin-Kreuzberg. Foreigners are German Turks, Turkish children who were born, raised and went to school in Germany; perhaps they speak German with an authentic Munich dialect, but travel with a Turkish passport and feel like tourists in their 'native country' of Turkey. Strangers are Afro-Germans who are 'German' in their language, their identity or their preference for German Christmas and German food. Yet in a very important social aspect, they are not 'German' – they have black skin and are spoken to and treated as the average German speaks to and treats blacks: 'You understands?' (*Du verstehen?*) Strangers are also Chinese-Americans who are proud of their ethnic identity and have no idea about China, but who continually have to answer the question on the street where the next Chinese restaurant is.

Strangers are German Jews who marched with enthusiasm for Germany into the First World War, were killed and only now have been honoured by a German defence minister with a commemorative wreath. Strangers are also German Jews who, with their prized medals from the First World War pinned to their chests, were taken away to the concentration camps in disbelief that patriots could do this to fellow patriots. Strangers are people who in their self-understanding are Jewish, who feel estranged in Germany and Europe and get their (fragile) identity from this strangeness. One day they end up in China and discover to their amazement, even horror, that the category of the Jew is completely meaningless in China. There, they are thrown into the same big pot of the 'European' and the 'whites' as their German opponents, whereby they are caught in a difficult identity crisis.

On the other hand, an Afro-German writes,

> I always liked being a 'mulatto', even in the terrible times of National Socialism. I have been able to manage the black and white in me very well. I remember when a colleague once asked me during the terrible 1940s whether I was very unhappy having to live as mulatto. I said, 'No, you know, what I have experienced in my life because of my ethnic origin, you will never in your entire life experience.'[2]

Not unhappy, where being a stranger and being in a foreign country are the stereotype of misfortune. Jew, where one wants to be German. Jew and German, namely 'white' when one is in China. Spoken to like a Chinese when one considers oneself to be a true American. The assimilated Prussian in Munich, the Franconian who suddenly discovers that he is a non-Bavarian, that the Munich Bavarians exploit and indeed always have exploited him. What is the common categorical denominator here? Are there one or more conceptual characteristics which might identify this general assembly of implausibilities and people with multiple identities as sub- and intermediate groups of 'strangers'?

Indeed, that is exactly the case! To grasp the category of the stranger one must grow accustomed to contradictions.[3] In a general way, it can be said that the category of the stranger *breaks open from the inside the established categories and stereotypes of the local world (the world of locals)*. Strangers do not fit into any of the neat containers that they are supposed to fit into, and therein lies an extreme irritation. To put it in another way, strangers are those who actually should be excluded according to the stereotypes of social order. They are Jews when they should be German, and Germans when they should be Jews. They are happy where they should be unhappy (and vice versa). They are native-born or second-generation people, locals – although the locals exclude them as 'strangers'.

Just how much 'strangers' are locals, neighbours, in their own self-image – although these locals are out to get them and they themselves have to fight against them as enemies – is made vividly clear by Jean Améry in his book *Jenseits von Schuld und Sühne* (Beyond guilt and expiation). He writes about an incident when he was a member of the resistance to National Socialism:

> One day it occurred that the German living under our hiding place felt disturbed by our conversations and carrying on during his afternoon siesta. He came upstairs, pounded hard on the door, stomped through the doorway: of all people, he was an SS man with the black lapels and woven symbols of the security police! We were all deathly pale with fear because in the next room were the tools of our propaganda work, which – unfortunately! – was not much of a threat to the permanence of the Reich. The man issued his command, and what for me was actually the most terrible thing at the time – in the dialect of my own home town. I hadn't heard this intonation for a long time, and therefore the crazy desire arose in me to answer him in his own dialect. I found myself in a paradoxical, almost perverse, emotional situation of trembling fear and at the same time of surging familial warmth. (Amery 1977: 85)

This example refutes a conceptual stereotype often considered essential to the category of the stranger, even in scholarship, namely the opposition to locals. There are endless variations of the claim that a mutual identity formation for both social and political action exists in antithetical terms such as 'us–them' or 'locals–strangers'. At the same time, the category of the stranger is confused with the category of the foreigner. Foreigners – French people, English people, Indians, South Africans – even when they are among us, know where they belong. They obey the rules in a world order of nation-states. Strangers are, on the other hand, French, or Africans, *in our country*. They are neighbours. Above all, they are near. 'I don't have anything against strangers. My best friends are strangers. But this stranger is from here,' says Asterix. The category of the stranger means: the distancing of nearness through closeness, which need not by any means result in mutual understanding.

Georg Simmel writes of strangers:

> The unity of nearness and remoteness is to be understood in the sense that distance means that he who is close is far and strangeness means that *he who is far is near* . . . The inhabitants of Sirius are not really strange to us, rather, they do not exist for us at all, they are beyond far and near. The stranger is an element of the group itself, like the poor . . . (Simmel 1950: 402–3; emphasis added)

This nearness of the stranger presupposes (relatively) quiet and orderly 'local' ways of life; only then is the stranger 'the wanderer who comes today and stays tomorrow' (p. 402). To put it another way, in a mobile world there are, if we think things through, ultimately either no more strangers or all are strangers.

Strangers are therefore neighbours of whom it is said that they are not like 'us'! By category, strangers are a double provocation: they are locals; and yet they do not obey the stereotypes which locals develop and maintain for themselves.

Hazel Rosenstrauch reports on how easily errors can occur, in the sense of an irony of reason, when locals describe the characteristics of their localness:

> At the beginning of the Third Reich, when Jewish children were still allowed to attend the regular German schools, there were stories again and again about how during school a child would be presented as a demonstration object and the characteristics of the Nordic race explained from his physiognomy, and the students could only hold back their giggling with great trouble because the SA man had called upon a Jewish child . . . It must have been difficult to believe in the superiority and beauty of the Aryan race in the face of a Goebbels, Goering, or even a Hitler. (1988: 32)

Neither nearness nor the particularity of the particular is natural; they must be socially constructed in the face of contradictions. A woman speaks German with a Munich dialect and has black skin. Therein lies a further irritation: if a black woman from Munich is not only possible, but actual and living, her mere being, her existence alone, refutes the naturalness of the limits and stereotypes on which locals have built their social world and order. Strangers are, in this way, a living refutation of the apparently clear borders and natural foundations through which affiliations and identities are expressed in the nation-state.

Closely connected to this second characteristic that strangers are the embodiment of exclusion and of existence between categories, a third characteristic presents itself: the *relativity* of the strangeness of strangers. Whether something or someone is perceived as 'strange' from their own or another's perspective depends in a banal, or perhaps not so banal, way on the frame of reference of the truisms which are taken for granted. Each person has only to pass through some boundary in order to change into the situation of the stranger.

There are natives and foreigners, friends and enemies – and there are strangers who do not categorically fit into this model, who dodge, obstruct, and irritate oppositions. The relativity of the stranger exists, as is clearly seen here, because the stranger is a *concept without a counterconcept*.

The report of an Afro-German on her attempt to discover her identity in Africa illustrates the extent to which race is a social construction:

> While taking a walk on the beach I saw children who were obviously looking for something of value in the piled-up garbage. They called out to me 'Whitey, Whitey' and I was once again stamped and felt branded. I had believed that I could appropriate a black African identity, yet this time I was yelled at as though I were white. I was stunned and couldn't speak to anyone about this. Only much later did I find an explanation for this incident. My behaviour, the observing distance, had betrayed me; at every scene I was either too aloof and or too interested to pass for a native inhabitant. My conduct marked me as a European. Because in clichés Europeans are white, at this point I became a white person. In this case white was a social category, not unlike how it is with the classification for 'black'. (Wiedenroth 1992: 169ff.)

The German black is slandered as white by African blacks. This reversal shows exactly what the relativity of the stranger means, but it also makes clear how little the stranger and strangeness can be conceptualized and identified in a natural or biological way.

How is this result to be understood theoretically? Reinhard Koselleck proposes that, in the field of political action and political history, we differentiate between *symmetrical* and *asymmetrical counterconcepts*. Among the former, he includes general comparisons like friend and enemy; the latter include asymmetrical antitheses such as Greek–barbarian, Christian–heathen, superman–subhuman. Thus these counterconcepts are characterized in that their opposite is contrary in an unequal way. One can and must ask here how the opposite standpoint – barbarian, heathen, subhuman – is negated in each case.

In my opinion, it is important to recognize that the category of the stranger precisely *evades* these counterconcepts. Koselleck differentiates conceptual orderings of the social: one symmetrical, the other asymmetrical and hierarchical. The category of the stranger, in contrast, negates *every kind* of conceptual ordering.

Strangers are not, at least from the perspective which I have presented here, the counterconcept to the concept of locals. Strangers *are* locals (neighbours); and they are at the same time in certain respects (sometimes from their own perspective, sometimes only from the outside perspective of the locals) also not locals. Put generally: the category of the stranger is *the counterconcept (or contrary concept) to all concepts of social order*. And therein lies their irritation and provocation, even as a concept.[4]

The entry into this point of view is the realization that strangers are not just foreigners of some nationality or other who cling to the stereotypes of the nation-state order. To put it provocatively, even enemies are in a certain respect less threatening than strangers because they obey the established order of the stereotypes of self and other. 'By their sheer presence,' writes Zygmunt Bauman, 'which does not fit easily into any of the established categories, the strangers deny the very validity of the accepted oppositions. They thus deprive the oppositions of their "natural" character, expose their arbitrariness and lay bare their fragility' (1990: 55). In other words, strangers are good evidence that the 'naturalness' of the local order is artificial and conventional. Through the contradiction which they embody (measured against prevailing images of the self in the social world), strangers demonstrate again and again that the world could also be different.[5]

That strangers are locals and not just strangers, as the locals think, is recalled by Michael Landmann: 'Not even the rudiments of Jewish religious practice existed in my family . . . that which we had been made into by three generations [of assimilation] determined us more strongly than our distant faded origin, which we knew only intellectually. We were Jews in a more pronounced way in the eyes of the world than in our own . . .' And he continues: 'After Hitler's insane slaughter of six million Jews, I was only one thing: a Jew . . . Levity was recovered only with great difficulty, trust in life and humanity never were fully recovered . . . one thing, however, remained for us: no law denies us our deeply painful love for German ways' (Landmann 1978: 116, 120ff.).

I repeat this sentence, 'no law denies us our deeply painful love for German ways.' Strangers are *ambivalence as existence*.[6]

To clarify and explain the category of 'the stranger', one must, at least, refrain from the current practice of equating and forcing into line strangers with foreigners and asylum applicants, and the disparaging connotations which result. Strangers can be the enrichment which again and again bursts own-group borders and narrow-mindedness. They awaken curiosity and open new worlds and perspectives. This is true even on a banal level: the Thai restaurant around the corner and the tourist trade are a 'strangers industry'. They market strangeness, live from the collective wish to refresh oneself during 'the best days of the year' in a foreign country as though at the fountain of youth.

Germans are ambivalent: they are especially willing to donate money for people from other cultures and countries who need assistance, for instance, the German Aid to Russia campaign in the winter of 1992, where entire trains full of donations rolled eastwards with public sympathy – while other Germans threw Molotov cocktails at helpless victims they labelled 'strangers'. Sometimes the two meet in one person. Someone who has just raided their own clothes cupboard for the Russian winter aid then mobilizes against the residence of asylum-seekers in their neighbourhood. How does this fit together? Two social types of relations intersect here: the distant needy 'foreigner' and the 'stranger' with official claims to welfare benefits in one's own neighbourhood. The readiness to help increases geometrically with distance. Jealousy and hatred of strangers increase proportionally as strangers lose their strangeness and, unlike the numerous tourists, are experienced as competitors for meagre state entitlements.

To summarize, the peculiarity of the concept of 'stranger' is that it is *a concept without a counterconcept*. Strangers are thus *not* just determined by the fact that they can be demarcated from others; they are determined much more by the fact that they undermine and crack open from inside all polar categories of social order. Strangers are neither enemies nor friends, neither natives nor foreigners; they are near and not near, far yet here; they are neighbours, who are excluded by neighbours as non-neighbours, as strangers. The strangeness of strangers appears frightening *and* enticing.

Strangers are at equal distances from knowledge and unawareness because they are simply *there*, present in their own horizon of knowledge and perception. But the strangeness of strangers at the same time presupposes a sweeping ignorance. The behaviour of strangers is stereotypically traced back to de-individualized characteristics of the collective: *the* Turks, *the* gypsies, *the* Jews, women in general, and so on, but not to the individual motives, reasons, circumstances and history of the person. One's own behaviour and the behaviour of one's peers are, equally stereotypically, understood and explained individually. Each man or woman acts here as a person and not as a representative of the collective.

The list of oppositions can be extended, but the fundamental principal remains: the particularity of the category of the 'stranger' is not expressed within the oppositions of social order, but lies in the opposition to all oppositions, which in turn does not recognize any opposition. The category of the 'stranger' means, in other words, falling between two stools: ambivalence as existence.

II

This definition of the stranger as ambivalence still presumes a relatively simple world. First, there is an 'us' here that can be distinguished more or less clearly from 'them'. Second the 'locals' have an absolute majority. Strangers are a 'negligible' minority, in both senses. This is what

I shall call the constellation of *simple* modernity. The social construction of the stranger is performed here in contexts of relative clarity. The 'locals' have their place in the structure of social order, from which 'strangers' must be distinguished and excluded.

Precisely this structure of borders and affiliations, normally conceived of in terms of nation-states, is being undermined and changed domestically and abroad by processes of 'reflexive modernization'. On the domestic level, own-group identities – regional, national and individual – are becoming indistinct, dubious, and being re-blended by a variety of mobility processes; abroad, there is the growth of multi- and international situations and interconnections, from business to information networks and telecommunications to natural destruction and the cross-boundary traffic in pollutants of the air, water and foodstuffs. This stage, in which modernization is changing the overall conditions and the ordering categories of industrial-society modernization, is what I call 'reflexive modernization'. What it means can be clarified theoretically by three principles.

First, *'manufactured insecurity'*, a theorem that does not necessarily mean that our existence has become riskier on an individual or collective level. The origin and scope of risk have changed, however. The consequences of technical and industrial development call into question the standards according to which they have so far been handled (the key phrase: beyond private insurability). Manufactured insecurity is not just a result of human intervention in the social and natural conditions of existence. This intervention violates the 'safety compact' that supported industrial society's consensus on progress.[7]

Second, such perilous situations provoked by civilization itself can no longer be understood or overcome locally or nationally: *'globalization'*. This is not or at least not only an economic phenomenon, and it would be wrong to equate globalization with the advent of a 'world system' or a 'world society'. Following Anthony Giddens (1990), I take 'globalization' to mean *actions at a distance*: a development which emerges from the transformation of time and space by global communications media and mass-transportation capabilities. Not only are global networks formed in this manner; local and personal horizons of experience are broken up and changed from the inside out. Our daily activities are more and more influenced by events that happen on the other side of the earth. Conversely, local lifestyles have worldwide effects and find worldwide dissemination. Globalization in this sense is a complex process which generates conflicts and new boundaries. Thus the appearance of local nationalism and the articulation of local ethnic identities can be understood as a consequence of the globalization which seems to contradict them. This correlation is currently observable in Russia.

Third, *detraditionalization and individualization*. What is meant by this is the exhaustion, dissolution and disenchantment of the collective and group-specific sources of identity and meaning (ethnic identity, class consciousness, belief in progress) of industrial society which, until the 1960s, had safeguarded Western democracies and economic society. The consequence is that all attempts at definitions will be imposed on the individual himself or herself. That is an essential aspect of 'societal individualization'.

What distinguishes this 'theorem of individualization' from the parallel interpretations which Georg Simmel, Émile Durkheim and Max Weber presented at the beginning of this century? Today people are being released, *not* from the security of status and religious cosmology *into* the world of industrial society, but from the industrial society of the nation-state into the turbulence of global risk society. People are facing a life with a great variety of contradictory global and personal risks (Beck and Beck-Gernsheim 1996).

Individualization does not just mean the dissolution of tradition; it also enables the invention of traditions. The idyllic – grandma's apple cake, forget-me-nots, communitarianism – is experiencing a boom.

Manufactured uncertainty, globalization and individualization can be developed in this sense as factors of a theory of '*reflexive modernization*' (Beck 1996; Beck et al. 1994). What is meant by that is not reflection on modernization, but 'reflexivity' in the sense of unintentional, often unseen, calling into question, changing and cancellation of modernization by itself. Modernization undermines and changes the premises and background conditions of industrial-society modernization along the lines of manufactured uncertainty, globalization and individualization. These have one thing in common: they emerge from the continuity of simple modernization and are thus part of the tradition of classical sociology, but along with the foundations of industrial capitalism in the nation-state, they undermine the foundations of traditional sociology and its controversies. Paradoxically enough, sociology might become the antique shop of industrial society because of the modernization of modernity, for which conventional sociology has lacked appropriate concepts and theories.

Under the conditions of reflexive modernization, the social construction of the stranger can no longer rely on the cultural self-understanding of a closed social circle; the definition of the self becomes particularly problematic. Individualization means, after all, that the culture of one's own group fragments and becomes more differentiated. A person born in East Frisia may go to school in Münster and Hameln, work in Bamberg and marry someone from Freiburg, while her husband pursues his career in Leipzig. They spend their vacations in Tenerife or in the Greek islands, and professionally they are extensively involved with both Scandinavian and Eastern European countries and languages. That is to say, individual existence is a mobile existence of tied-down rootlessness, synchronically and diachronically throughout the biography.

Sighard Neckel puts the consequence in these words: 'That which Georg Simmel considered the characteristic of the stranger – "the wanderer who comes today and stays tomorrow" – is about to become the ordinary way of life in the age of individualism' (1994a: 47f.).

In other words, reflexive modernity generalizes the category of the stranger; one of its central characteristics is *universal estrangement*. More and more people are losing their unambiguous social position. Identities become mingled. Boundaries no longer hold. People live with strangers, to whom they are also strange. 'Modern society is able to generalize estrangement only because it simultaneously abolishes the special status of being a stranger by making *everyone* a stranger. Paradoxically, everyone can be a stranger only when there no longer are any strangers' (Hahn 1994: 162). The question is therefore no longer how we deal with strangers, but how strangers of various sorts deal with one another. And, how does the category and condition of the stranger shift when it is universalized?

For instance, Erving Goffman (1967) has studied the universalization of strangeness. He speaks of how, with the pervasion of modernity into people's everyday relationships, 'we' and 'they', mistrust and fear, give way to something that might be called *'civil inattention'*. This is, moreover, a highly active attitude that must be carefully constructed, maintained and balanced out.

In multinational, multilingual Switzerland (perhaps an exemplary country of generalized strangeness, a mini- or pocket Europe), people speak of 'tolerant ignorance' or 'ignorant tolerance'. This is certainly also an essential reason for the moral indifference with which many people allow public excesses and violence to happen. It is also a highly fragile behaviour pattern, which is based on mutuality and can be practised only to a limited extent in the increasingly violent metropolitan jungles.

III

Does this mean that the relationship to strangers is becoming unproblematic? No, the opposite is true. The consequences of reflexive modernization demonstrate this in detail. Individualization also means that own-group identity becomes blurred. Globalization means, among other things, that the walls of distance break down and that strangers and strangeness are increasingly caught in the horizon of one's own life. Manufactured uncertainty means that danger lurks everywhere and no one does anything about it. *One* possible consequence is that many people experience their own global world as threatened by universal strangeness. All levels and corners of society mobilize against this. It boils down to a question of concern to all of society: the *politicization of the question of security.*[8] Strangers do well in unfamiliar terrain, advises Ronald Hitzler, to confront what threatens them '*with* rather than *without* prejudices'.

> Cutting oneself off, locking oneself in, hiding – these are today's most common ways of reacting to the fear of the things happening 'out there' which seem to threaten us in a variety of masks. Deadbolts on the door, entrance locks, multiple security systems, alarms and surveillance cameras have spread from upper-class villas to middle-class areas. Living behind a wall of mechanical locks and electronic walls, whistles, pepper sprays, tear-gas guns or tazer guns is part of individual urban survival orientation (1994: 58f.; see also Hitzler 1999).

There is an emerging multiculture 'of egoism, ethnocentrism, narrow-mindedness, mistrust, jealousy, grumbling, demands, objections; a multi-culture of active boundaries and of ignorant intolerance' (Hitzler 1994: 58f.). This, however, *changes the context, actors, agencies and resources of the social construction of the stranger.*

'For some time,' reports Agnes Heller from the United States:

> a 'race rhetoric' has replaced the rhetoric of the 'social question', which means that for questions of race, definite rules of the game have also been institutionalized. These institutional rules of language for race and gender questions are even obligatory in the private sphere. Not even in one's own apartment, with friends, should one use forbidden words or tell jokes (about blacks, Jews, homosexuals) because it could be falsely interpreted. And whoever is reported can easily lose their job . . . Only the self-representation of a group is regarded as a legitimate form of representation of this group. Any representation by another (for example, the representation of blacks by whites, of women by men, homosexuals by heterosexuals) is by definition regarded as 'racist' and 'sexist'. The only legitimate contact between races (and genders) is struggle; the alternative to that is mutual self-isolation and its normalization. The modern racists repeat the old racist arguments: the other cannot feel as we do, he has another epistemology, he cannot ever understand what we think, how we suffer (under him) and so on. MacKinnon, who considers censorship the key to rectitude,

'knows' (from where, one would like to ask) that men (of course, only men) consume pornographic products, and think about pornography even while they are teaching. Call in the thought police! (1994: 25)

The new making of boundaries in the world, the separation and fortification of 'us' and 'them', is being managed with the means and authority of *civil society*, so to speak, as a global citizens' initiative under *subpolitical* direction:

> It's about discipline and punishment. And it's about monitoring. Sexuality, habits of speech, behaviour and forms of representation are all monitored – down to the smallest detail, if mis-steps can lead to the loss of a workplace, media, exhibition space, etc. Some time ago now, when barely anything had been said to this effect, Foucault remarked that the most devastating discourse of power of our time was not initiated by the modern state, but rather produced and directed by the power and authority of 'civil' society. Civil society turns out to be completely uncivil. (Heller 1994: 26)

In Europe, where society never dominated the state, but instead the state dominated society, we are coming to a change of scenery and strategy: to put it simply, from culturally to bureaucratically constructed strangers. In contrast to the 'cultural stranger', the 'bureaucratic stranger' is not vague and categorically incomprehensible. He is not originally a bureaucratic, but a cultural category. The new German hate term 'Asylant' comes to mind as an example.[9] This term (which has no equivalent in English – the language of the United Nations speaks simply of 'refugees') originates in administrative, legal and official German. An 'Asylbewerber' (political asylum applicant) is differentiated from an 'Asylberechtigter' (person entitled to political asylum). These are officially defined groups of strangers put away in barracks. It is interesting that the term 'Flüchtling' (refugee) is reserved for Germans in the juridical and political language of the Federal Republic. A 'Flüchtling' is by definition German. Diana Wong writes:

> For lack of a precise juridical and sociological possibility of definition, the term 'Asylant' runs amok, as it were, in social discourse. Who is meant by this remains unclear and contradictory. Different answers are available: recognized asylum applicants, or non-recognized asylum applicants, or all asylum applicants, or perhaps all foreign refugees. What is meant by this status also remains unclear and contradictory: genuine victims of political persecution, refugees fleeing from poverty, economic refugees, foreign criminals, black drug dealers. Its semantic power is increased by the

numerous suggestive, catchy phrases which on closer inspection, however, prove devoid of content. The term 'asylum-seeker' serves as the root for combinations such as: flood of asylum-seekers, stream of asylum-seekers, asylum-seeker catastrophe, asylum-seeker tourism, and pseudo-asylum-seekers. The shortening of the term 'Asylanten' to 'Assi', also slang for 'Asozialer' [deviant], is the next logical step. (1992: 410f.)

The experience of locals with 'asylum applicants' is officially mapped out and organized. It includes the Office for Foreigners, the Social Security Office, the Residents' Registration Office and so on, but above all, the apartment buildings and temporary shelters assigned to them in people's neighbourhoods.

The field of foreigners' and refugees' rights anticipated something which threatens society in general, 'the new politics of the strong state' (Heribert Prantl):

the word 'organized crime' functions like a conceptual master key that unlocks everything – every taboo, every fundamental right. The system of legal protection built in the last forty-five years is being weakened. Areas of 'discretion free of judicial interference' are being promoted, not only in criminal law, but in administrative law as well. Conservative politics considers complete democratic control a restrictive subordination. Fundamental rights apparently become invalid whenever the strong state thinks it is 'better off' without them . . . (Prantl 1994)

This means that the models of perception and action in risk society are transferred to the 'risks of civilization in a liberal democracy' (Ronald Hitzler). A general suspicion of anomie takes the place of ecological dangers. If in the latter case the foundations of industrial production are being renegotiated, the same goes for the foundations of a liberal constitutional state in the former case:

Politics is in the process of developing a new state. In the security state of the year 2000 the point will no longer be tracking criminal offences and preventing concrete dangers, but avoiding even conceivable risks. In this state every single citizen will thus be considered and treated as a risk factor. Such a state, conceiving of itself as an organization to avoid risks, will leave the population fewer and fewer freedoms. Their anxiety about crime, just like their anxiety about refugees, is a state-promoted anxiety. The result is that each state measure meets with general approval so long as it promises more security. The people in such a state believe that they are for the time being in a well-guarded vacation club – and only notice too late that it is a luxury-class prison. The type of 'public spirit' conservative politics has recently demanded means the renunciation of individuality and the rights of the individual. (Prantl 1994; see also Hesse 1994; Ewald 1993a)

IV

One can glean an essential consequence from the previous arguments. Those, like Karl-Otto Hondrich (1994), who reduce the eruption of violence and renationalizing tendencies in Europe to a background of oppression, ethnic identity, popular culture or language commit at least two category mistakes. First they *essentialize* cultural identity, and second, they confuse it with the *calculated power of enemy stereotypes*. This conceals a principal objection to the in-group, out-group logic which is characteristic, not only of sociobiological and ethnological theories of aggression and conflict, but also of social theory from Émile Durkheim through Georg Simmel and Max Weber, all the way to the group theories of interactionism and existentialism. It does not imply anything about the social construction and dramatization of *specific* enemy stereotypes.

In this sense, it is necessary, in conjunction with the question of how images of strangers are culturally, socially, politically or bureaucratically constructed, to distinguish between (everyday) *stereotypes of the stranger*, on the one hand, and *enemy stereotypes* on the other hand. The question that this difference justifies, is why are only particular cultural identities and *not* others dramatized into national and state enemy stereotypes? And why do stereotypes of enemy and ally often change so quickly? Thus, in prerevolutionary America, the British 'motherland' (possessing the same language, same ethnic identity, same politically republican fundamental convictions) was the 'natural enemy', while later, in the twentieth century during the Second World War, it was the 'natural ally'. What is regarded in a certain social space, a certain epoch, as 'ours' and 'strange' is not natural, but rather an empirical and historical question which is difficult to foresee and forecast.

Gottfried Benn makes a note under the heading of 'the contents of history':

> In order to inform myself, I open an old school book: the so-called 'small Ploetz'[10] . . . I open at any page, say page 337, concerning the year 1805. There one finds: one naval victory, two cease-fires, three alliances, two coalitions. Someone marches, someone forms an alliance, someone unifies their troops, someone strengthens something, someone advances, someone captures, someone retreats, someone captures a camp, someone resigns, someone is awarded something, someone inaugurates something brilliantly, someone is a prisoner of war, someone compensates somebody, someone threatens somebody, someone marches to the Rhine, someone marches through the Ansbach area, someone marches to Vienna, someone is pushed back, someone is executed, someone is killed – all of this on one single page – the whole thing is without doubt a pathological story of madmen. (1989: 362)

Exactly this 'pathological story of madmen' *refutes* the conclusion of a sociobiologically (ethnologically or anthropologically) diagnosed conflict potential belonging intrinsically to the respective squabblings or battle formations. German emigrants, for instance, who came from the feudal restrictions and apprehensions of Europe, lived in the United States on good terms with blacks, embraced mixed marriages and suffered and defended an originally democratic country in which slavery was at that time protected. There is no way of drawing a conclusion as to the social history of enemy stereotypes from the sociobiology or sociology of social in-group or out-group stereotypes. These must be viewed and understood in the context of the state, the nation-state and the military, that is, in their significance for the state's monopoly on power.

And yet, to this very day, the old legend has maintained its bloody power: what is one's own must be marked off against that which is alien in order to obtain and retain its identity. One could call this the *territorial* theory of identity. It alleges the existence of a space defended by (mental) fences so that self-awareness can become possible. Yet when one separates this notion from the context in which it arose, the nation-state, it loses all plausibility. This error, which has been codified many times and has already become tear-stained history, could be called the *prison fallacy* of history. It is not necessary to lock people away from one another, not even in the ample spaces of a nation, to guide and organize them against others, for them to become confident and sure of themselves. That is a superstition of modern people; it is doubtful whether others subscribe to it. Why should it be possible for people to meet and confront one another with a sense of identity and security only in the prison cells of states? Opening these and letting the 'prisoners' mingle offers a wealth of material and opportunity for finding and forming identity.

This reveals another cognitive error, as Zygmunt Bauman, in particular, has pointed out: the delimitation logic of identity remains trapped in the metaphysics of non-ambiguity that inspires modernity. Identity is imagined to be *unambiguous*, an either-or, with the middle excluded. The possibilities of an ambivalent identity, of achieving and constructing something of one's own by mixing diversity and strangeness, remain almost completely ignored (Bauman 1992). This prison-like theory of identity has scant appreciation of the wealth which others can mean for the self and its transformation into the other.

'Enemy stereotypes' are dramaturgically enhanced and legitimated, culturally generated (usable) prejudices and stereotypes of others that are functionalized for the construction and expansion of the state power and military apparatus. Enemy stereotypes, in contrast to mere stereotypes of strangers or racial prejudices, make it possible to re-evaluate values. Here it is possible and even necessary (in the event of war) to kill. There is no mediation agency and no court for enemy stereotypes. Enemy stereotypes represent a second para-, extra- and even antidemocratic source of legitimation for the modern (nation) state. As legitimation becomes more difficult, this source becomes more attractive to the agents of the state.

The consequence is that we are cut off in culture and in social science from recourse to traditions or ethnic identities for legitimating strangeness and in-group/out-group differences. In other terms, *ethnicity is not an axiomatic variable of social differentiation; it is a thoroughly political and bureaucratic construct* (Neckel 1994b). It is not justified to make a leap from cultural difference, varying perceptions of the stranger and the self – no matter how these may be defined – to varieties of political dramatization and the construction of stereotypes of strangers and enemies. These stagings *use* nature, heritage, original and substantive things as cover, but they carry out decisions, selections and constructions which are tantamount to inventions.

In reflexive modernity, the construction of strangeness is doubly politicized. First, the politicization of the question of security mobilizes the control instruments of civil society and of the strong state. Second, the figure of the bureaucratically (constructed) stranger replaces the cultural stranger. The discourse of cultural difference is energized into a discourse about enemy stereotypes intended to legitimize the construction and reinforcement of the preventative security and protective state.

The usual talk of the in-group/out-group logic in many theoretical and research traditions of the social sciences (and sociobiology) *hides* this process of selection, origin and politicization. A critique of the system-theoretical discussion of exclusion/inclusion would have to start here as well. Using the generality of ideas, this latter discourse suppresses the nastiness of particular processes of separation within the administrative and political system and the public media. It conceals the important part intellectuals play in the foundation and preparation of the legitimation models from which the silhouette of the stranger can be manufactured and mass-produced. This selection process can be seen even when the in-group/out-group relationships are equated with national identity (patriotism, nationalism). Why not combine regional identities with a European self-consciousness? Why not mix, for instance, Franconian separatism with professional pride and a civilized identity that derives its self-consciousness from the affirmation of technical and legal rationality? I am not saying that everything is combinable. Yet I wish to say that, given the duplication, individualization and globalization of the social worlds in which individual lives are involved, an almost inexhaustible mosaic of possible exclusions exists. So it is naive (perhaps strategically so) to speak about 'inclusion' and 'exclusion'. The question is instead the unity of difference between inclusion and exclusion.

That is the horizon which opens the inquiry into the social and political definition and construction of strangeness and enemy stereotypes, both socially and politically. It does justice to the reality of the cultural potential for violence without, however, falling into a political fatalism. Quite ordinary public, political and administrative construction processes – and their prevention – become the centre of attention. As previously stated, neighbours *become (are made)* into Jews. This 'are' is first of all not passive, but meant to be active. Secondly, it certainly excludes the past tense 'became' (were made); it is aware of actual threats and it appeals, thirdly, for the early, joyful defence and development of an open society and the liberal constitutional state.

11

Nation-States without Enemies: the Military and Democracy after the End of the Cold War

Anyone who has an explanation for the present day is suspicious. We are experiencing times which are irritating to the point of inhibiting thought. Still, I would like to ask: what relates the peaceful revolution in East Germany, the decay of the Soviet Union, the Yugoslavian drama, the reforming of the German military and the approving, onlooking, indeed passive complicity of an unfeeling majority in view of brutal offences against human rights in Germany? My tentative answer: these are symptoms of a new type of phenomenon, the *state without enemies*. This is not a state without enemy stereotypes, but rather a state in search of the lost enemy. My question is this: what theoretical and political perspectives result from this state without enemies, the most recent offspring of a long militaristic history?

The German Minister of Defence, Volker Rühe, recently remarked that 'Germany is encircled by friends.' 'Encircle' fits superbly, because a country born of the former West Germany and East Germany, both built up on enemy stereotypes in the East–West antagonism, must experience this new lack of enemies as deeply upsetting. Moscow wants to enter NATO. The former Volksarmee is serving with the Bundeswehr. Communists proclaim allegiance to capitalism. At the same time, to be sure, there is shocking news of civil wars, there are nuclear weapons floating around freely, armies without states, new states with unclear boundaries sharing armies, and so on. It is as if history had never opened a sociological textbook. These are the consequences of the collapse of a global order. This deep uneasiness cannot and must not conceal one thing: Western Europe at least is without external enemies. The pogroms against foreigners are also a reaction to this lack of enemies. This is unparalleled in history.

All states, as the British sociologist Michael Mann has calculated, spent half of their time throughout history making war (Mann 1984: 31). The gamut runs between one-third (Prussia) and two-thirds (Spain from 1476 on). The eighteenth century was extraordinarily bellicose, while the nineteenth was unusually peaceful. The twentieth exceeds all previous centuries in the horrors of war, and now comes this Maximum Credible Stroke of Luck, the emergence of the state without enemies in Europe. What kinds of contradictions erupt along with this abrupt transition from a front-state democracy to a democracy without enemies. Three theories mark out the horizon.

First there is the early bourgeois theory of *pacifistic* capitalism (Comte, Schumpeter). It asserts that the conquest of world markets is superior to all other conquests. In the past, warlike peoples conquered trading peoples, but today the converse is true. East Germany's joining of the Federal Republic of Germany is the most recent example. Furthermore, business fosters international trade relationships which undermine and overcome nationalistic narrow-mindedness. Capitalism is therefore a school of cosmopolitanism.

By contrast, second, theories of *militaristic* capitalism point out the coexistence of war and world trade up to the present day. Industry has profited from war and war from industry. As everyone knows, the world wars broke out between highly developed industrial states. And the so-called warlike states of the Middle Ages were virtually pacifistic if one takes as a standard the horrendous military budgets in what Schumpeter calls the 'essentially non-militaristic' modern states.

This widespread theory that war, the military and arms build-ups are an integral necessity of capitalism overlooks what Martin Shaw (1988) calls military socialism, 'the socialism of total war'. The Soviet Union and Eastern Europe became communist essentially as a consequence of the First and Second World Wars, not (as Marxist theory would suggest) due to industrialization in the individual countries. Weapons and not arguments, the soldier and not the proletarian were the basis for the victory of 'real socialism'.

Third, I would like to develop the theory of *militarily bisected modernity*. This adopts theories from both of the two previous versions, but makes them relative and links them in terms of social theory and social history. Allow me to state three theses in advance:

1   Democratization *and militarization* took place roughly in parallel in the nineteenth century. Enemy stereotypes also integrate modern society, limit democracy and enable governmental action.
2   The Cold War was a system of *de*nationalization of the nation-states. Paradoxically enough, the nuclear build-up enabled a demilitarization of society.
3   In the state without enemies, the contradictions between militarism and democracy burst out. The individualization of the welfare state, thought out to its logical end, neutralizes the defence emergency. In that way, early bourgeois theory is now regaining theoretical and political importance in the form of an involuntarily pacifistic capitalism.

A word on the conditions of application: I am speaking in essence of the countries in Western Europe. For the countries of the former Eastern bloc, modifications apply which I cannot expound here.

Sociology of the enemy stereotype

The revolution leading to modernity – the abolition of feudal governmental forms, the replacement of a divinely ordained order by one ordained by people, with a parliament, division of powers, a government that can be voted out of office – all of these achievements were established in the nineteenth century together with the extension of military service to all citizens. Universal suffrage and universal military service (both for men) are twins born at approximately the same time. Likewise, the expansion of industry went hand in hand with the industrialization of war-making. Weapons production became mass production. The creation of transportation systems served both civilian and military planning. The contradictions between political and military mobilization were made virtually unrecognizable by the internal presence of an external agency: enemy stereotypes.

In all previously existing democracies, there have been two types of authority: one coming from the people and the other coming from the *enemy*. Enemy stereotypes empower. Enemy stereotypes have the highest conflict priority. They make it possible to cover up and force together all the other social antitheses. One could say that enemy stereotypes constitute an alternative energy source for consensus, a raw material becoming scarce with the development of modernity. They grant exemption from democracy by its own consent. Modernity also perfects the military form of the self-legitimation of power and bureaucracy. The military, the defence emergency and so on are thus not merely geostrategic and foreign-policy concepts. They are also aimed at an internal, non-military, militarily approved organizational form of society in all its parts: production, work, law, science, internal policy and publicity. In other words, all democracies are militarily divided democracies. The military consensus limits the democratic consensus and vice versa. Fully established democracy cancels the willingness to participate in a defence emergency.

I do not know whether it is possible to survive the experiment of modernity, the entry into the roller-coaster of innovations, *without* enemy stereotypes. In fact this intermingling of democratization, industrialization and militarization has become routine and continues to be practised. The connection between nationalism and political emancipation becomes comprehensible if one relates the concentration of power in the state, the lack of any higher authority, that is, national arrogance and arbitrariness, to the revocation of the old social order in perpetuity, which is precisely what that concentration accomplishes. This is the origin of the integrative central state that exercises the monopoly on the right to use force, finances its standing army and bureaucracy with taxes and creates a uniform law and educational system inside its boundaries. The dialectic of military threat and resistance justifies the construction of a power apparatus in a several ways: as mobilization of consensus in domestic policy (less euphemistically, as a whip making it possible to tame the simmering industrial class conflicts), and as a spectacle of preparation for and waging of war. No matter how bitter this insight may seem, the threat of wars stabilized the world of primary industrialization.

An extraordinarily important characteristic is that the power for self-affirmation is inherent to enemy stereotypes. Enmity arouses enmity. Enemy stereotypes irritate, mark others off, insult, prepare for violence and generate angst until what they speak of actually happens. Neighbours, people of different languages and from different cultures, first become strangers and then enemies. Enemy stereotypes have the terrible power of being self-fulfilling, because they set in motion a mechanism of resistance and response which, in its anticipation of anxiety, only provides new nourishment for all sorts of anxiety. 'In the beginning was the Word.' This verse from the creation story probably does not apply anywhere with such terrible directness as in the world of violence created by the word 'enemy'.

This reality-creating power of enemy stereotypes is the other side of state sovereignty. When neighbours quarrel, the police come and a judge mediates and pronounces a verdict. Feuding states are everything at once: prosecutors, perpetrators, judges and executioners. The lack of any separation of powers in the relationships of states to one another makes enemy stereotypes so powerful in reality and so bellicose because states that are in conflict cannot be brought to their senses by the dispassionate objectivity of agencies and rules of procedure.

A comparison to the modern love relationship forces itself upon us here. Like detraditionalized love, which does not know or recognize any decision-making agency above itself, enmity is highly susceptible to interpretation. Even disruptions of communications can have devastating consequences in the event of a conflict. But the difference between private marriage and wars between states is that states can justify their actions circularly. They take the stage with and brandish all the insignia of legitimacy. They always have *their* law, their parliament and usually their public on their side. As the Sophists already recognized, justice and power are often synonymous in this cynical sense. That is why the role of the elites and the mass media in the social construction or destruction of enemies is so important. Enemy stereotypes are intellectual weapons or metaweapons: words, in whose horizon violence comes to be taken for granted. They make it possible to shift things that have been produced internally, at least in part, on to something external. The other, the stranger, the enemy is guilty, where all the other external factors – God and nature – slip away.

Sociology of the Cold War

The Cold War – it can and must be said in retrospect – was a gift from God. It gave order to a world that had skidded into the atomic age, an order of terror to be sure, but one that made it possible to shift internal crises off on to external causes, that is, enemies. The Cold War implemented a divided global society based on enemy stereotypes. Please spare me the Cold War nostalgia! Yet we must be permitted to inquire into this clock that made the world tick and see how it operated.

Soviet imperialism was also a boon to the West. For one thing, it cooled down a classical source of unrest in Europe. Just how much the communist dictatorship eased life for the West is becoming clear today, when neither the EC nor the UN is able to put an end to the military conflicts in the shattered former Yugoslavia. Soviet imperialism managed, for its own imperialistic interests, what the West can no longer accomplish.

Moreover, *socialism was presented to the world as imperialism*, an experiment in voluntary self-refutation. The fact that the West became anticommunist is a gift of Eastern communism. Before the Second World War there were strong socialist and communist movements in the highly developed industrial states. After the Second World War the East became

one big proof that capitalism is necessary, a proof that was never con-
clusively produced in and by capitalism, with its crises and tendencies to
disintegration.

The Soviet rockets produced the West. Sociology has so far conducted
research largely under the assumption that national boundaries are also
causal boundaries. The Cold War, however, can be understood only as
a boundary-spanning causality. Internal features of the West – specific
aspects of the party landscape, the social structure, law and the attitude
of citizens in quite different types of countries – are also a product of
the Eastern threat and its domestic and foreign policy stage management. Many so-called inherent developments of 'advanced industrial
society', of 'late capitalism', of the 'welfare state', of 'postmodernity'
will probably prove in the future to be a product of the Cold War. The
tendency of heterogeneous states and traditions in the Western camp to
become more similar, in any case, indicates the overarching compulsion
to denationalization. This can be illustrated by the example of the self-
standardization and self-Westernization of left-wing opposition parties:
the SPD (Social Democratic Party of Germany) became 'fit for government' only *after* its Bad Godesberg oath to the Western alliance and the
latter's economic rules of the game. 'Ostpolitik' was only able to take
off under Western sails.

The West was a system of semi-sovereignty, of self-limitation and
self-disempowerment of national sovereignty, not from conquest, as
in the East, and not from values, agreements and markets either, but
because of the omnipresence of the communist peril as constructed and
presented for domestic purposes. Seen from the opposite side, it may
be that an essential reason for the destabilization of the Eastern bloc
was the loss of its enemy stereotype, or even more, the transformation
of that stereotype into an ideal under the influence of Western mass
media.

Recent activist movements (with opposite opportunities for development in the West and the East) arose precisely against this consensus
and compulsion to form blocs. Those movements are the children of the
Cold War.

Thus the Cold War impressed its order of terror on an unstable Europe,
an order which has now become mere scrap paper. There no longer is a
European security system, since the contractual parties to the agreements no longer exist, nor do the political territories to which they
referred, nor do the interests which they were intended to balance out.
It remains to be seen whether treaties, European institutions, markets
and the 'Democratic International' can be compelling enough *without*

common enemies to tame the centrifugal forces of the world economy, national egoisms and the elective affinities and antipathies of history.

The East–West antagonism was a collective consciousness in Durkheim's sense, even a global consciousness, which organized thought and action everywhere on earth. Modernity thus also generates its antithesis: an anticivilization of violent conditions, based on enemy stereotypes and the nuclear threat, that cast a spell over the entire world.[1]

The end of the defence emergency: the individualization of society

As paradoxical as it may sound, the nuclear arms build-up permitted a demilitarization of society. Technology replaced human labour. Electronic war-making became a matter for technicians. The arms build-up consumed resources such as money, technology and knowledge, but it also permitted a demobilization, even a civilization, of society. This is how militarization and democratization can be advanced *simultaneously*.

I would like to interpret the theory of individualization in this context. The dynamic of individualization in the welfare state also breaks up the last bastion of large-group society, the enemy stereotypes, just as it does with class cultures and the nuclear family. Everyone has an enemy, but for that very reason it is no longer the shared, integrating enemy. The thesis is this: *individualization cancels the defence emergency* (in the orthodox foreign policy sense of Carl Schmitt). The civilization of culture happens unintentionally, as the side-effect of a deep-seated transformation which sociologists associate with the division of labour (Durkheim), the inner-worldly asceticism of Calvinism (Max Weber) or the finance economy (Marx, Simmel), but as I have attempted to show, it has taken on a special character and become permanent in the development of the welfare state since the sixties. With advancing individualization, it is becoming true for the first time in history that 'states that bark don't bite.'

Even though single-person households by now constitute over 50 per cent of those in large cities, individualization does not mean many things – atomization, autonomization or isolation – that some wish it meant in order to refute it more easily. Individualism means, first, the *dis*embedding of traditional collective ways of life and second the *re*-embedding of ways of life in which the individuals must sustain themselves and cobble together their biographies, even inside nuclear families.[2] The search, even the craving for, collective identities which we are currently experiencing does not contradict individualization, but is in fact a product of individualization gone pathological. On the one hand, people revolve about the axis of their own life under the dictates of market conditions. On the other hand, some romanticize the family, while others invoke decline, discover the esotericism and the identity of things that are clear and simple, fight a bitter battle against the devil or profess with aggressive joy: 'I'm proud to be a German.' However one might evaluate this process, a great variety of contradictory things are emerging here, but certainly not a new unity. The balance of terror has been replaced by the *balance of complainers*: everyone is at odds with everyone and everything. This eternal strife, not eternal peace, now prevents the grand consensus of the defence emergency.

Applying this to a contemporary issue, one often hears that a professional army would alleviate the legitimation problems generated by any operation of the Bundeswehr outside our own boundaries. That is probably an illusion. Imagine this: the old Bundeswehr had all the advantages of consensus on its side, in its mission of defence against a visible, identified 'arch-enemy'. In an operation outside German national boundaries, all the obviousness of defence is lost. Attacks, even if they occur within 'peace missions' (best regards from Orwell), must be justified in a cross-fire of criticism. This presumes that yesterday's trading partners can credibly be fitted into the role of villains. The objectives of such an undertaking always remain complex and controversial, and all of this occurs in a country which (if public opinion research does not deceive us) would like to become a Green republic or, more precisely, a *Green greater Switzerland*, in a world that is still sitting on a nuclear powder keg. If you ask me, this is the Maximum Credible Dissent perpetuated.

By comparison, the old '*domestic*' Bundeswehr was a biotope of consensus, even a source of consensus that could refresh others. The new 'global' Bundeswehr will be the exact opposite, a source of unquenchable strife. The consent of the political parties to an amendment of the constitution is one thing. The other problem is whether the Bundeswehr is even capable of consent. The prognosis of individualization theory is negative. Each mission will subject the country to a new internal ordeal.

To put it once again clearly: it is anomie, not pacifism, which prevents the defence emergency. Risk society is socially explosive even in calm times. When this is combined with the collapse of a global order, turbulence of all sorts, including violence, becomes possible. Trying to combat this by staging unstaged we-feelings (Karl-Otto Hondrich) is to engage in black romanticism. The new apostles of community from the United States, the communitarians, are also preaching instead of analysing. That is the flight to an ideal world generated by the defective real world.

The state without enemies and its futures

The fat years of the Economic Miracle in Germany went hand in hand with a political starvation diet. Politics shrivelled down to social policy. Western Germany had settled into the sunny corner of the East–West antagonism and was happily occupied with its harmlessness, its renunciation of force, its high marks for democracy, its legendary efficiency and thereby its second, technoeconomic conquest of Europe. These fortifications of apoliticism – moralism and a peace policy – collapsed with the fall of the Wall.

The former West Germany was not a political structure in the sense of claiming and fulfilling a policy and sovereignty of its own. One can certainly say that this apoliticism of the former West Germany was the basis for its morality. The Germans were able to be so virtuous because they let their flags wave politically in the Western wind. Their lack of sovereignty justified and permitted an economic ambition that clad itself in general good will. Their professions of peace originated de facto from the morality of impotence. Now all of that has suddenly collapsed. The turns of phrase are still alive and, amidst the spreading anxiety and helplessness, they are in fact being passed around like relics that give a second life, but they no longer create any reality. Western policy, too, has lost its rudder, compass and lighthouses. The former West was shattered in the victory, and amidst its rubble such antiquated, forgotten and repressed things as national interests, geopolitical situations, separatism, mistrust, borders that keep people out and must be defended in emergencies are beginning to form themselves over again. What is needed is nothing less than to recast the political slogans of the postwar era, such as 'War should never again start from German soil', into new forms of policy to foster and preserve peace.

It is not just Germany's neighbours who are afraid of an economically powerful Germany in the national squabbling of a still-fictitious Europe. The fear of Germany on the part of foreigners is perhaps exceeded by many Germans' fear of Germany. Just as the German communists dreamed up a constraint system built on education and surveillance to free the Germans from the Germans, many now seek refuge in Europe from the resurrection of a past that can become possible only through a sovereign, economically powerful Germany in the centre of Europe. This comparison and parallel between the transplanted anti-fascism of the former East Germany and the flight of *nouveau riche* Germany to Europe is certainly unfair. One reason is that there is ultimately no alternative to a European confederation for the nations of Europe. Yet the strange phenomenon remains that the Germans want to move into the newly constructed European house for fear of themselves, while conversely the other nations fear the sacrifice of their sovereignty.

A spectre is haunting Germany and this spectre is called Germany. This existential nervousness, this mingling of hate and fear, this uncertainty about one's own possibilities and abysses also explains the cowed tension with which people tolerate fire bombs in hostels for foreigners (which those young old Germans also throw into the nation's repressed memories), as if the onlookers were paralysed. The victorious powers were more than that; they were also protectors or self-protectors of Germany, or more precisely two Germanies, from itself. In the place of the old protective powers, Europe thus becomes a self-protective power which is to protect the Germans from Germany.

In dealing with the 'asylum-seeker problem', conversely, there is the stimulating experience for many Germans that 'we're so terrific that we have to defend ourselves against the influx from all over the world.' Understood in this way, xenophobia is not just an emotion of people under pressure, but also the enjoyment of the Germans' repressed and mangled national awareness of being able once again to look down on others in grand style.

Politics, frozen in East-West oriented thought and action, is being thrown into a new system of possibilities. Five scenarios, not mutually exclusive by any means, can only be pointed out here:

1   In search of the lost enemy;
2   Involuntary pacifism – the 'demobilization' of front-state democracy;
3   Ecology as grand consensus – from the state without enemies to the ecological state;
4   The new nationalism and the principle of self-determination;
5   The round-table state – the subpoliticization of society.

1   In search of the lost enemy

Lack of an enemy does not mean lack of an enemy stereotype. On the contrary, it creates an unquenchable need for new enemy stereotypes. Who can deny that bloody conflicts are breaking out everywhere after the end of the Cold War? It is noticeable, however, that precisely in a country which for the first time in its history finds itself 'encircled by friends', such a lively trade in all possible and impossible enemy stereotypes should be flourishing with eager participation by intellectuals of all convictions.

The trend runs from the concrete to the interchangeable enemy. First, there is the *mobile* enemy: the grand enemy is replaced by interchangeable enemies of the moment (Islamic fundamentalism, the Third world,

Iraq, Serbia and so on). Second, while governments or religions may be the point of focus here, as *abstract* enemies they are replaced by diffuse collective groups (asylum-seekers, foreigners, migrants) or even general ills of modernity (drug trafficking or organized crime). Third, a moment-ary enemy gap can always be replaced, ultimately, by reconsidering the fundamentals, for instance, by presenting hostilities as insuperable. This *anthropological* flexibilization of enemy stereotypes makes it possible to have enemy stereotypes without enemies. The more irrevocable and impenetrable the threat, the larger and more varied will be the future markets for security and military technology around the world.

2 Involuntary pacifism

Frontline-state democracy could now 'disarm' domestically. For instance, the Radicals Decree[3] has become unnecessary and could be replaced by its opposite: a decree attracting people with civil courage, people willing to rethink things, people able to combine fantasy and realism, into the civil service. Part of this is that the left is rethinking its enemy stereotype of capitalism. The criticism of 'late capitalism' (which has almost become early again) becomes more mobile and effective if that phenomenon is not demonized as the source of all evil (nationalism, militarism, patri-archy), but instead its ability to learn is discovered. Then the agenda of the future – ecological reform, feminist restructuring and the civilization of militarily divided modernity – will become politically redeemable and shapeable.

3 From the state without enemies to the ecological state

If enemy stereotypes are reduced there is the threat of disintegration. As chance would have it, however, a new source of consensus is coming into existence for developed modernity: the *grand ecological consensus*. It shares the class-spanning nature of the former defence consensus and even enlarges it into a supranational dimension. The state without enemies could undergo a metamorphosis into an *ecological state*, not only to save nature, but also to provide governmental-political action with consensus and a future. The ethic of self-limitation which the ecological issue anchors in people's hearts can also be utilized for other fields of policy, such as limits on the welfare state and control of costs in health care.

A business sector that discovers the global market for ecology and is able to learn from it splits up. This split in turn permits the construction of learnability by political means. Just as the petty princes were played off against one another by popes and emperors, the distribution of win-ners and losers initiates a power play involving business sectors, firms, taxes and regulations. This makes it possible to enter into alliances and to play one force off against another. In short, a brief handbook of *ecological Machiavellianism* could ease and accelerate the transition from ecological morality to ecological politics.

4   The new nationalism and the principle of self-determination

With the weakening of the centralist state apparatus built on force, core political concepts change their meaning. The example of this with the most power for the future is probably the *principle of self-determination*. This principle, smirked at by many as a relic of an antiquated bourgeois ethic, is proving after the demise of the military blocs to be a sharp, two-edged sword in the relations among the countries of Europe and the world. Things which could previously have been done only with war, such as shifting the boundaries between states or cancelling the balance of power in an entire hemisphere, are just as thoroughly and peacefully achievable today by claiming and putting into practice the fundamental democratic right to self-determination for ethnic groups and parts of states. If one keeps in mind how even Western states were held together by the external pressure of the communist threat, then one can imagine how the centrifugal forces of ethnic autonomy can and will gain dynamism. Even the old large states of Western Europe – France, England, Belgium, Spain, etc. – may soon fall under the knife of the principle of self-determination which they honour. Perhaps a European mosaic, a European power puzzle that increases the number of states on the political map of Europe, will arise from this confusion.

If even the monopoly on the means of force is loosened and those in social conflict arm themselves, a horror scenario results: the *Lebanonization* of large parts of the world.

5   Subpoliticization of society

In a state that loses its specific characteristic, the 'intimate relationship to force' (Max Weber), politics is reopened, but outside the political system. The weakening of the state goes hand in hand with a strengthening of other social actors, the mass media for instance, but also of organizations, occupational groups, citizens' initiatives and so on. The 'de-statization' of the state means two things. First, there is a 'subpoliticization' of society, and second, this may imply in the most favourable case the invention of the negotiation state, the *round-table state*, where domestic and international conflicts are discussed.

This can be clarified by the example of the economy. The militarily inhibited state reaches for the weapon of the boycott and thus makes the economy the continuation of war by other means. But, given the mobility of enmities, this leads to a domination of international trade relations by foreign policy from the top down.

'Wishes for Germany' (I quote Gottfried Benn from the year 1942):

> redefinition of the concepts of hero and honour. Elimination of any person who says Prussianism or *Reich* in the next hundred years. Leave the administration of history to mid-level bureaucrats, but place it under a European executive body with regard to direction and principles. Have children between ages six and sixteen raised according to their parents' choice in Switzerland, England, France, America or Denmark at state expense. (Benn 1989: 366f.)

In my view, one should add: vacations on the Starnberger See are possible.

12

Brief Introduction to Environmental Machiavellianism: Green Democracy from Below

The environmental crisis is in crisis. Someday someone will attempt to establish a career by demonstrating that it only ever existed in people's heads, that it was a hysteria of the seventies and eighties when the world still made sense – in the environmental crisis. Pension provisions and global apocalypse were the main problems of those brilliant years in the sunny corner of the East–West conflict. Now, when everything is beginning to wobble, we have 'real' problems. Some scientific 'counterevidence' would be welcome indeed.

But even these are symptoms of the victory crisis of the environmental movement. Everything that becomes established begins to wear down. 'I have reached the conclusion that we must take a bold and unequivocal action,' writes Al Gore, by now the Vice-President of the United States, 'we must make the rescue of the environment the central organizational principle of our civilization' (Gore 1992: 270). How are we to understand this? How might it become possible? The environmental movement must break out of the eggshells of its technical and moral self-concepts and organize itself as a political movement. Or, to put it another way, it needs tutoring in 'environmental Machiavellianism'.

Two (bitter) confessions or insights open the way. First, there is no *environmental* movement. Second, there is no natural nature. The two have something to do with one another.

Nature as utopia

'Once again I realized what a humbug nature is,' writes Gottfried Benn:

> Snow, even if it does not thaw, scarcely provides any intellectual or emotional motifs; one can completely master its unquestioned monotony intellectually even without leaving the house. Nature is empty and deserted; only Philistines project something into it, the poor souls, always going on and on. Forests are completely unproductive; everything below 1500 m is passé now that they can see and experience Piz Palü for DM 1.00 [in films] ... Flee from nature! It botches thoughts and is notorious for ruining style! *Natura* is naturally a feminine term. Always out to draw off semen, coitizing and weakening the man. Is nature natural at all? It starts and lets go, beginnings and just as many interruptions, turns, failures, abandonment, contradictions, revelations, senseless dying, trials, games, semblances – the textbook example of the unnatural! Besides that, it is still uncommonly laborious, uphill and down; slopes that even out, outlooks that cloud over, lookouts which were formerly unknown and are again forgotten, in short, nonsense! (Benn 1986)

What does the apparently quite natural word 'nature' mean? Rural life in the fifties (as it now presents itself in hindsight or as it presented itself in those days to someone living in the country, or to those dreaming of a life in the country, or to ...)? Mountain solitude before there was a book entitled *Hiking in the Lonely Mountains*? The nature of natural science? Nature as the opposite of chemistry? The highly polished network models of ecology? The nature of gardening books? The nature one longs for (in the sense of calm, a mountain brook, inward meditation)? Is it nature as offered in the tourism catalogues of the global solitude supermarkets? Nature as a feast for the eyes? The beauty of a hilly Tuscan landscape, a highly cultivated art of nature? The rain forest? A zoo without bars?

Thus nature is not nature, but rather a concept, a norm, a recollection, a utopia, a counterdesign, and this is more true today than ever. Nature is being rediscovered and coddled at a time when it no longer exists. The environmental movement is reacting to the global condition of a contradictory fusion of nature and society which has sublated both concepts in a mixed relationship of mutual interconnections and injuries, for which we do not yet have an adequate conceptualization. In the environmental debate, attempts to use nature as a measuring standard against its own destruction fall victim to a naturalistic misunderstanding. The nature to which they appeal does not exist.[1]

Environmental Red Cross consciousness

Al Gore is certainly not the first environmentalist, but he may be the first one to create and forge politics from the environment. At least in the programmatic sense. What he promises to draw on is the power of the environmental issue to create meaning, policy and structure. It only seems as if the post-traditional world is disintegrating into anomic individualities. Paradoxically enough, in the challenges of self-induced endangerment, it also possesses an inexhaustible source of remoralization and motivation: namely, neuroses. To put it pointedly, Al Gore replaces status and class consciousness, belief in progress or in doom and the enemy stereotype of communism, with the 'human project of saving the environment'. In a 'New Deal' that would have seemed mere dreaming until recently, ethically conservative, religious and left-emancipatory ideas and tendencies are reconnected and allied in this project – and they stimulate the economy. In any case, industry in the United States defected to the Democrats at least partly because of this environmental moral policy and its economic promises.

The environmental crisis generates and cultivates a cultural Red Cross consciousness. It transforms everyday and trivial matters into tests of courage where heroism can be displayed. Far from intensifying and strengthening the meaningless spiritual emptiness of modernity, environmental hazards create a substantial semantic horizon of avoiding, depending and helping, a moral climate that intensifies in tandem with the size of threat, a climate in which the dramatic roles of heroes and villains take on a new everyday meaning. Sisyphus legends emerge. Even negative fatalism – 'nothing works any more, it's all too late' – is ultimately only a variant of this. This is the background against which being a Cassandra can become a vocation or a career.

The perception of the world in the coordinate system of ecological-industrial self-imperilment turns morality, religion, fundamentalism, hopelessness, tragedy, suicide and death – always intermingled with the opposite, salvation or help – into a universal drama. In this real-life theatre, business is free to take on the role of the villain and poisoner, or to slip into the role of the hero and helper and celebrate this publicly. The cultural stages on which the environmental issue is played out modernize archaism. There are dragons and dragon-slayers here, odysseys, gods and demons, except that these now respond to chemical formulas and are played, assigned and refused collectively in all spheres of action, in politics, law, the administration and, not least of all, in business. In the environmental issue, a postmodern, jaded, satiated and fatalistic culture of luxury creates a Herculean task for itself, which acts as a stimulus everywhere and splits business into 'villains' and 'Robin Hoods'.

The results turn often enough into grotesques. The urban planners at the Technical University of Berlin inquired into what environmental action means in everyday terms: 'abolishing fireworks, reintroducing chamber pots, cooking with less water, using candles rather than light bulbs, turning off the lights in shop windows, ironing only those items of clothing that are visible, abolishing cobblestones, prohibiting smoking . . .'

Schwabach, a small city near Nuremberg, was recently selected by the Federal Construction Ministry as an 'ecology' city. Minister Irmgard Schwaetzer handed out the prize personally. 'The Holluba family', reports Michael Mönninger in the *Frankfurter Allgemeine Zeitung*, 'which was chosen the "most environmentally aware household", promised to continue purchasing food only from organic farmers, to wear natural clothing, to eat whole foods and as little meat as possible, to collect rainwater and use low-consumption toilets, to drive a car only with at least four people aboard, to go on holiday by train and to go hiking' (1993: 29).

So Benn once again correctly sensed what was coming when he described the German future: 'Small housing estates, tax-subsidized sexual intercourse in the dwellings, home-pressed rapeseed oil in the kitchen, home-made pancakes, regional clothing on their backs, grey flannel, gymnastic bars in the yard and midsummer bonfires in the hills – that's your full-blooded Teuton' (quoted in Mönninger 1993).

Democratization of rubbish

The power of environmental morality to shape politics can be designed, not at all coincidentally, by a comparison with the national consensus in matters of defence.

Environmental morality and the consensus on defence approach salvation from the now anonymous, universalized and objectified 'enemies', 'enemy substances' that is, with equal fervour. But while the consensus on defence has something like conscientious objection, an objection to environmental service seems to be out of the question. Young and old, even managers and government officials, but above all women, are compelled to lend a hand in this daily defensive battle.

The national security consensus still has peacetime. Ordinarily, the 'defence emergency', war, remains a mere threat, and that alone accomplishes a great deal. Its executive powers are limited socially and temporally, however. The environmental issue, if it ever came to power, would be a kind of permanent wartime, if one will permit the analogy. Action is imperative, immediately, everywhere, by everyone and under all circumstances.

One need only recall the humble patience with which the democratization of recycling is endured and carried out today in order to recognize what a structuring power lies in the environmental issue. Reckless industry has turned all of us into unpaid field labourers recycling for it. The motto seems to be: if production is not to be democratized, then at least its waste products can be. We do not reject this with screams of outrage (and appeals to the polluter-pays principle), but comply around the clock with masochistic industriousness. No one has a rubbish-free day anywhere, and even more peculiarly, no one is calling for one. That, among other things, shows how profoundly the environmental crisis, as internalized culturally, has already changed and politicized the entire society.

The environmental social conflict

Increases in welfare and hazardousness condition one another. The more that people become (publicly) aware of this, the less defenders of safety can continue to sit in the same boat as the planners and producers of economic wealth. The old 'unpolitical coalition for progress' between administration, the state, business, technology and politics shatters because while technology may indeed enhance productivity, it also puts legitimacy at stake. The legal order no longer fosters social peace because, in tolerating the hazards, it also universalizes and legitimizes disadvantages and threats to life.

Industry and economics become a *political* undertaking in the sense that large investments presuppose lasting consensus, which is now endangered rather than guaranteed by the old routines of simple modernization. Things which it has so far been possible to negotiate and execute behind close doors in the form of 'objective exigencies' – organizational and personnel policies, the range of products to be produced and the 'unintended consequences' of hazardous production processes – all of these must now face the crossfire of public criticism.

In short, a novel symbiosis of economics and politics arises: the unpolitical bourgeois of late capitalism as regulated by the welfare state becomes a 'political bourgeois' who must act and prove himself in the economic sphere as well as in his electoral district. That does not mean that the entrepreneur or executive becomes an elected representative. The neutral indicators of profit and income still decide on the success of production and investment, but the concrete question of 'how' becomes political, controversial, codeterminable and capable of consent, even in need of it. That is another reason for the 'new sanctimoniousness' of business: enterprise ethics, enterprise culture, the magic word of 'self-responsible' group work and experimental attempts to go 'beyond hierarchy'.

The powerlessness of official politics against the industrial bloc only applies to the classical setting. It can be overcome in a politics of politics that advances and develops its opportunities in forging environmental alliances. In its dual function as consumer and conscience, the public is thus permanently forced to become the father confessor for a sinful business sector. Things that had thus far existed only on paper and had not been taken seriously by anyone – monitoring, safety, or protection of citizens and the environment from the destructive consequences of economic growth – suddenly become levers with which the state, the public, citizens' groups, the administration and the law can plan and execute their political intervention in the strongholds of business in the name of a new environmental crusade.

Losers generate winners. As industry publicly loses its environmental innocence, other business sectors build up their 'greening' livelihood. As we noted in the preceding chapter, an economy that becomes capable of learning environmental lessons will divide. This division then makes it possible to learn by political means. The balances between winners and losers open up a political game involving industrial sectors, companies, taxes and monitoring, spiced up and prepared with 'scientific risk analyses' that pass the buck of causality back and forth. This 'game', which originates along with politics itself, makes it possible to forge coalitions pro and contra and to play them off against one another in order to re-politicize politics. Thus it is possible to give tutoring to an environmental policy in the form of a pocket handbook of environmental Machiavellianism. Only this latter takes away the air of technological naivety from the slogan of an 'environmental renovation of industrial society' and equips it with the political significance and power to act that are becoming necessary in the transition from environmental morality to an environmental politics.

The outlook for environmental politics

In systematic terms, one can distinguish two constellations in the environmental conflict, following the schema of Volker von Prittwitz (1990). The first constellation is blockade, where polluter industries and just the affected groups confront one another in spectacular fashion. This begins to change only in a second constellation, in which helper interests awaken and the cover-up coalition between polluters (the chemical industry, for instance) and losers (the tourism sector, for instance, whose customers stay at home in view of polluted oceans) begins to crumble. This occurs as parts of business, but also of the professional intelligentsia (engineers, researchers, lawyers and judges), slip into the role of rescuer and helper, that is to say, they discover the environmental issue as a construction and expansion of power and markets. This, in turn, presupposes that industrial society becomes an industrial society with a bad conscience, that it understands and indicts itself as a risk society. For only that allows helping and coping industries and careers to develop themselves and their heroism, which both motivates and skims off profits. This presumes abandoning mere criticism and turning to the siege of the status quo by alternatives. The environmental issue must be broken down into other questions: technology and production design, product policy, form of nutrition, lifestyles, medical diagnosis and precaution, legal norms, organizational and administrative forms, foreign policy and development policy.

Only a society which awakes from the lethargy and pessimism of the confrontational constellation and conceives of the environmental issue as a providential gift for the universal self-reformation of a so far fatalistic industrial modernity can exploit the potential of the helping and heroic roles and gain impetus from them to actually ensure viability in the future, rather than just indulge in cosmetic ecology on a grand scale.

Ecology abolishes the neutrality, the objective apoliticism of the economic sphere. The latter splits up in its sinfulness on the level of the personality and identity of people at all levels, all the way into the management elite. This susceptibility to division into the sinful and the redeemed permits a 'political sale of indulgences' and restores to politics the power instruments of 'papal sanctioning and prohibition', the public exhibition and self-castigation of the great industrial sinners, even the public torture implements of an 'environmental inquisition'. Most politicians shy away from this in their publicity-conscious kindness. But this need not continue to be the case forever.

Does this mean that 'with the danger, salvation comes as well'? Certainly the converse is also true: new dangers threaten from the salvation. Very contrasting social structures and models of order can be forged from this moral and political material: democratic ones and dictatorial ones, to mention only the extremes. There is probably no political tendency that could not draw honey from the environmental issue. The environmental issue is a political chameleon which changes its appearance as it is put into service. That is precisely the reason why the issue of environmental democracy, which tames the countermodern, dictatorial potential, combining and reconciling it with the doubt of modernity, is so important and so urgent.

13

Freedom or Survival: the Utopia of Self-Limitation

Once upon a time, two or three decades ago, the bothersome question that comes up sooner or later for every new generation, 'now what do we do?', could be answered quite simply: 'the same as always, only in grander form', two cars instead of one, telecommunications instead of telephones, genetically manipulated nature and human nature instead of farming and animal husbandry. This was called, peculiarly enough, 'faith in progress'.

This 'golden' age of prescribed thoughtlessness is over. It has given way to the depressing discomfort of a generalized helplessness and lack of foundations. Today, people have to mull everything over, negotiate it and justify it, and still they are suspended over an abyss. No one ultimately knows how things will continue. Everything is possible, but nothing seems to work any more.

Take transportation as an example. It is possible to reach almost any corner of the world in the briefest time. Yet the more this advances, the more nothing seems to work any more: congestion. As the possibilities increase, it simultaneously becomes impossible to question or reform the social and economic foundations of universal mobility. Not even tens of thousands of people killed and maimed each year were able to make people stop and think about the traffic situation, much less provoke a political storm of outrage over it. Only the realization that modern automotive rootlessness is tantamount to a self-endangerment of civilization (smog, the hole in the ozone layer, destruction of forests, climatic changes) was able to create the small-scale utopia of a car-free city – without results so far.

Industrial modernity is a human machine gone wild. It breaks all taboos, but declares a taboo on the foundations that make this giantism and this general violation of taboos permanent. The triumph of this creed of 'bigger, faster, more' for everyone and in all fields has finally made this contradiction clear and problematic. Just imagine that everyone had a second car. Heaven on earth for the automobile industry, but hell on earth for everyone else. Who is fighting for the 'common good' here? What does 'duty' mean in this context? If extended to the entire world, the Western model reveals itself as a suicidal project. It amounts to self-destruction, or at least self-obstruction, perpetrated in plain sight. This insight generates and nourishes the opposing view, the demand for self-limitation, and the questions, 'how are we to understand that?' and 'who is standing up for it?'

Congestion has become a metaphor for the involuntary politicization of modernity. It symbolizes the coerced utopia of self-limitation. Congestion means the involuntary sit-down strike of everyone against everyone else, technically imposed mass Buddhism, an egalitarian forced meditation for drivers of all classes of cars. 'You're not caught in the congestion, you are the congestion' is written in large letters in a tunnel. Thus congestion becomes the characteristic of an entire culture. This does not mean just traffic congestion, but the obstruction of modernization in general. The linear modernity of 'bigger, faster, more' is at risk of breakdown everywhere. This applies, as we have found out by now, to the ecology, but also to the welfare state, wage labour society, the transportation system, the pension system and so on. The implacable 'more' and 'faster' of simple modernity is colliding everywhere with the problems, erosion and obstacles it generates: destroyed nature, empty coffers, more demands and fewer jobs despite, or perhaps because of, the economic upswing and economic growth.

We have been living for some time now in an industrial society with a guilty conscience. One could even speak of a civilian desertion from the missionary consciousness of modernity's faith in progress. If people are still in favour of progress, then it is only in hopes of preventing something worse: loss of jobs, loss of world market shares, loss of comfort and convenience, etc. All that remains of the missionaries of progress from primary modernity is the residual affirmation of double negation, the justification of the lesser of two evils. This recalls the reservations expressed by party cadres just before the collapse of East Germany. The crucial difference is, however, that for the new Germany there is no West Germany to turn to. There is a lack of an alternative.

The search for one has been underway for some time, however. The pleasant interlude without a utopia is coming to an end. One need only say it openly for the scales to fall from everyone's eyes: we are living in the precursor stage of a new reformation, including the associated religious wars. Marx only appears to be dead. He has come back to life as an executive, a Green, an activist mother and feminist, a microchip, a genetic therapist, a member of the 'revolutionary viruses', a futurologist, a guru of flexibility, a market anarchist, an apostle of unemployment and a fundamentalist of naturalness.

One need only look in the newspaper: full-page, high-gloss advertisements in which arch-industrialists proclaim their morality as Green converts. Even if not a word of this is true (which I doubt) this still means that the semblance of a Green reformation is being, if not nailed to the church door in Wittenberg, at least published in the business section of the *Frankfurter Allgemeine Zeitung*. Turning the page, there are reports of conferences and conference results from the elite intelligentsia, which is apparently conferring non-stop and coming out with outcomes. Even great names (I am thinking, for instance, of former Chancellor Helmut Schmidt), exempt from any suspicions of revolutionary views if only because of their familiar toothpaste-white smiles, are announcing with unnerving insight that we are encircled by hostile global problems. Given the low birth-rates in the West, there is less and less talk of the 'population explosion' as the root of all evil, as if there were some connection between a baby and a bomb that would require one to jump for cover. Even the general complaint that nothing is happening only demonstrates the pressing belief that, finally, something ought to, has to happen. This widespread five-minutes-to-midnight feeling indicates the readiness for fundamental reforms (at least in someone else's front yard).

Thus it is no wonder that a 'commission on the future' was probably founded to make this very point publicly: self-limitation is not a negative, a residual or a small utopia but rather an undertaking, unparalleled in history, that is penetrating into fields not yet conceived of. Western industrial society itself must discover (or invent) a substantive limitation of its scope of action. This means, according to Kurt Biedenkopf: 'It must limit its social and individual action in a manner that is *narrower* than the bounds set for it by its techno-economic abilities.'

But in order that things should not become quite that bad, it evidently seems like a good idea to many to respond to the novel challenges with conventional plans and formulas: the state, the market, community. These are keywords that represent the political philosophies of Hobbes, Locke and Rousseau. These responses are 'conventional' because they are both thought out and obsolete. They are perfectly suited to be demonstration objects of what one should *not* do at the turn of the twenty-first century.

To call for a strong state is to presume a strong consensus, which is what that appeal is supposed to create or compel. State action in a modernity that is putting itself at peril is more, not less, dependent on active consent, which cannot simply be summoned, but must be won laboriously and purposefully. Anyone who reacts to conflicts over mega-technologies (research reactors, use of unproven technology) with the tactics of the police state will soon find this out. The demand for a strong state gets stuck and spins its wheels in the circular situation of having to rely on what is still to be achieved: an order capable of gaining consent.

The attempts of a neoliberal economic fundamentalism to take recourse in the self-restorative powers of the market are stricken with historical blindness. They have not even caught up with the recipe for success in Germany which is by no means new or secret, reading: only politically stable continued development towards a *socially just* free market economy can obtain and renew consent for the market. Anyone who expects everything good to come from all-round reforms of the 'community' – the keyword here being 'nation' – usually ends up sooner or later in a helpless political antimodernism, if not a forced communal-ization imposed by state terrorism. Another ridiculous historical incongruity: we are living in a globally active export economy which, at the very moment it switches over to worldwide communications, reintroduces the nationalist post-carriage, following the motto of 'on foot and horse-back into the one big world of the third millennium'.

All these attempts, moreover, are blind in one eye morally and politic-ally. People usually step on the accelerator with one foot while hitting the brakes with the other. More pointedly, many would like to reintro-duce corporal and capital punishment, bring back compulsory school prayer and see the prohibition of abortion enforced, but at the same time they idolize the thousand channels of banalization in private televi-sion, transporting violence into the last innocent nooks and crannies, as well as genetic technology and gigantic weapons technologies. In Bavarian terms, this amounts to a policy of yodelling high-tech.

All the neoconservative variants of a politics of self-limitation get caught in this contradiction. In the same breath, people want to be re-actionary in cultural and social policy and modernistic without restraint in economic, technology and military policy. They prefer to pass the buck of self-denial to *others* – women, the poor, modernizing countries on the way to being industrial – while sunning themselves in self-limitation by the cynical right of the wealthy and powerful to lift all restraints on themselves.

The key to self-limitation does not lie, therefore, in going back, in nostalgia or in regression as 'reform', as is currently being demanded everywhere. It is imperative to confront these neoconservative tenden-cies in all parties and in all social strata and camps with the transition from primary, industrial modernity to a second, enlightened, reflexive modernity. The challenges of a global modernity in a 'cosmopolitan intention' (Kant) will thus be understood and mastered only if they accept the achieved state of development, of democratic culture, legality, technological refinement and self-realization of individuals as their precondition. Self-limitation must be combined with modernity's claims to freedom and justice. Anything else is not only historically blind and ethically questionable, but also utterly unrealistic. It would be a bloodless, intellectual, test-tube politics that made its plans without taking into account the people and groups who are to support, affirm and implement the utopia.

But how does self-limitation as self-liberation become possible? It can be conceived of and developed (extremely tentatively) along the lines of the following principles: cheaper is more beautiful (more beautiful is cheaper), slower is more democratic, being more self-responsible is more fun. Politically, the federative idea (and not just for Europe) must be developed further. This ultimately involves limitations from an ethic of self-responsibility and self-organization. That only becomes possible, however, if hierarchies are broken up and interdependencies loosened. Precisely in globalizing modernity, something like clarity and tangibility of the consequences of one's own actions for others must be reconstructed. All of these principles – the construction of accountability, tangibility, responsibility, that is, slowing down because of democratization – can easily be traced back to the liberation from self-imposed immaturity in Kant's enlightened sense, except that the present critique is directed against industrial orthodoxy. More, not less, modernity beckons to us beyond industrial gigantomania. Hunger for freedom, not asceticism, leads us there.

Social, political and economic fields of action can certainly be 'reconstructed' in such a manner that the actors are forced into reflection on the distant effects of their action. Such a dilution of dependence is discussed in the social sciences under the keywords 'self-reliance' (sociology of developing countries), 'loose coupling' (organizational sociology) or 'decentralization' (political sociology). The shared fundamental idea here is to restructure fields of action such that the actors burden their environment less with problems of consequences and simultaneously become more autonomous in their decisions and responsibilities.

If one thinks along this 'rationality of shortened causal chains' (Claus Offe), then in the temporal dimension this means, for instance, that those alternatives whose possible consequences and dangers can be recognized early and remain correctable must be granted a bonus. This argues, for instance, against speeding the way to market for technological innovations, as is now being demanded everywhere, but for renewable energies and also for the mixing of functional spaces in city planning, for the combination of rights and self-obligations in old-age and health insurance, and so on. In the social dimension, something similar could be achieved by the expansion of basic rights, employment security or local autonomy and veto rights. This not only reduces the social unpredictability of centralist administration and management decisions, it also constructs self-responsibility. Perhaps it is the still secret elective affinity between democratization and deceleration, a clarified Western analogue to the experience of East Germany, which will free us from the orthodoxy of industrial modernity.

Notes

Chapter 1 Freedom's Children

1 Quoted in the *Frankfurter Allgemeine Zeitung*, 4 June 1994; in a letter to the editor of the *Süddeutsche Zeitung*, Kamphaus has subsequently turned against the misinterpretation of his essay as cultural criticism and pleads for an understanding of freedom's children. Cf. also ch. 3 below.

2 This view is also directed against the brilliant argumentation by Scott Lash in Beck, Giddens and Lash 1994, where Lash consistently inquires into the possibilities of post-traditional 'reflexive community formations', but does not mention or consider the ancient and highly modern tradition of a political Europe of individuals.

3 See, for instance, ch. 6 below.

4 See ch. 8 below.

5 See Wilkinson 1997.

6 Quoted from 'Opas Tante', *Der Spiegel*, no. 43 (1996), pp. 41f.

7 The example of the United States, however, that it is difficult to determine the limit where loss of membership (or failure to turn out to vote) becomes a threat to the continued existence of the political system.

8 Similarly, Warnfried Dettling (1994) describes how the 'culture of helping' has changed: 'The volunteer fire brigade and the army, parties and charitable organizations certainly still represent social activities, but there is a growing number of (young) people whose social commitment overshoots these offers and seeks other forms. They do not want to become the executive organ of some set ideal of service (Gerhard Schmidtchen). Today it is a different group of people who become social activists.'

9 Barbara Sichtermann in a commentary on North German Broadcasting (NDR), Hamburg, Sept. 1995.

10 See ch. 5 below; cf. also Dettling 1996.

11 'Increasing individualization does not demolish solidarity relationships whole-sale; rather, it creates a new type of solidarity. It is exhibited voluntarily

and not so much from a sense of obligation. It is also less inspired by a morally charged pathos of helping. The price of a high degree of self-determination and a diversity of opportunities appears to be a loss of orientation. This in turn leads to a demand for binding social networks that create a sense of belonging and a meaning in life' (Keupp 1995). For the discussion and misunderstandings (!) of the concept of 'individualization' see Beck and Beck-Gernsheim 1996.

12   Karl-Otto Hondrich and Claudia Koch-Arzberger write: 'But where the compulsoriness of power, the cold contractual character of the market, the emotional elevation of love and the kind condescension of unilateral help do not suffice or are not accepted and lose their binding force, that is where solidarity finds its place as a binding and regulating force of a unique type. More emotional than contracts but more sober than love, it does not dissipate itself in selfless charity, but assumes mutuality of support at least for an indeterminate future. It is inspired by the idea of some sort of equality between givers and receivers, despite the differences between them and their mutual distress, it originates voluntarily and can be dissolved the same way' (Hondrich and Koch-Arzberger 1992: 114).

13   From an interview on South German Broadcasting (SDR), 13 Nov. 1996.
14   See ch. 10 below.
15   Regarding this institution-dependent individualization, see, for instance, Beck (forthcoming); Giddens 1991.
16   On the contradictions of conservatism, see Giddens 1994.
17   *Leviathan*, no. 2 (1994), p. 283.
18   Immanuel Kant, *Zum ewigen Frieden*; quoted from Kant 1983: 207; emphasis added by Ulrich Beck.
19   See Beck 1996; ch. 8 below.
20   On controversies regarding the challenges of 'global society' and 'politics in global society' see the volumes to be published under the editorship of U. Beck in the series Edition Zweite Moderne (Suhrkamp, Frankfurt), as well as Albrow 1996a.

Chapter 2   What Comes after Postmodernity?

This is the text of the address with which I opened the Convention of German Sociologists in 1990 at Frankfurt am Main.

1   Approaches to this appear in Beck and Beck-Gernsheim 1995.
2   Hannah Arendt writes: 'The inexpressible cruelties of a spontaneous pogrom on a gigantic scale were too much even for the SS, in fact they gave it a bit of a scare; they intervened to stop the slaughter, so that the murder could proceed in the way they considered civilized' (Arendt 1979).

Chapter 3   The Withering Away of Solidarity

1   To clear up certain misunderstandings of the ambivalent concept of 'social individualization', see Beck and Beck-Gernsheim 1996; on the debate over

'individualization' see the collection of essays *Riskante Freiheiten* (Beck and Beck-Gernsheim 1994); for systematic analyses, see, among others, Berger 1995.

2   On this point, see Beck 1996, as well as ch. 8 below.

Chapter 4   Perspectives on a Cultural Evolution of Work

1   Thus there is a particular urgency today in Jean-Paul Sartre's (1974) quite general insight that 'so long as one does not study the future structure of a particular society, one runs the risk of not understanding the social at all.' The present chapter was first published in the mid-1980s and accordingly it contains no references to the explosion of subsequent literature on 'post-Taylorism', 'post-Fordism', 'lean production', the 'end of the division of labour', operational 'systems rationalization' and the resulting radical changes (and continuities) of industrial labour. It is likewise impossible to go into the subsequently published literature on individualization and wage labour (on this, see the articles by M. Kohli and M. Baethge in Beck and Beck-Gernsheim 1994: 219–44, 245–364).

2   In what follows this perspective is extrapolated in a *consciously oversimplified* manner. Without pursuing the multiple interactions between culture, work and the economy and without inquiring into the 'material contingency' of the sketched-out 'cultural revolution' and the 'social circumstances' behind it, three different developmental stages of the cultural system are analysed, very schematically, in their consequences for the structuring of industrial labour. This is not intended to assert that culture 'determines' work relationships (as is similarly claimed for technical and economic developments). Instead, one forgotten parameter of influence among the conditions that change it is to be recalled to consciousness. Cultural influences thus only become evident where the historic symbiosis of 'Protestant ethic and the spirit of capitalism' is breaking apart. In this sense, the thesis of a cultural evolution of labour, as asserted here for Germany, has also been developed for the United States by, for instance, Clark Kerr. Under the title 'The great American cultural evolution in the labor force', he illustrates with a great deal of supporting material the thesis that: 'A great cultural transformation in attitudes and expectations within the labor force accelerated in the 1960s and 1970s, but its origins antedate the past two decades' (Kerr 1979). See also the essay by Amitai Etzioni and especially that by Daniel Yankelovich (also in Kerr and Rostow 1979), in which there is an argument which is quite parallel to mine in sections II and III, although to avoid footnote-itis it is not always cited.

3   Alongside Weber and Veblen, one ought to mention Émile Durkheim and Georg Simmel among social scientists in this respect, and in the present day, John Kenneth Galbraith and Daniel Bell.

4   On this 'rehearsal' of the 'industrial virtues', see Vester 1970; Thompson 1963.

5   Pioneering works in this discussion include Inglehart 1977; Klages and Kmeciak 1979; as well as the thematically relevant articles in Matthes 1983. In recent years, methodological shortcomings in Inglehart's work have been pointed out, see, among others, Kudera 1982; Jagodzinski 1983.

6   This is presented in detail in Beck 1983; for corresponding developments in the working class, cf. Mooser 1983; in the feminine life context, cf. Beck-Gernsheim 1983; in the youth phase, cf. Fuchs 1983. The term 'individualization' is undoubtedly an enigmatic and easily misunderstood concept (on this see ch. 3 above, esp. its note 1). As used here, this term does not mean a generalization of the legendary 'bourgeois individual', but instead the break-up of class cultures that can actually be perceived socially and experienced. There is also a novel, sometimes much more direct and vulnerable, thoroughly contradictory societalization of the individuals under labour market conditions as protected by the welfare state; in this point see the cited references for details.

7   See Bahrdt 1975; Mooser 1983.

8   This becomes clear, to pick out only one example, in the enormous boom which 'environmentally friendly' and 'alternative' technologies have experienced in the past decade. On this phase of a 'self-reflexive modernization', which turns its own follow-on problems and risks into science, see, in general, Beck 1982.

9   On this, see, among others, Engfer, Hinrichs and Wiesenthal 1983; Inglehart 1977; Klages and Kmeciak 1979, including the corresponding data and tables, which will not be reproduced here.

10 From the flood of literature on this issue, let us point out in particular the volume on the future of work, *Zukunft der Arbeit*, ed. Benseler, Heinze and Klönne (1982), as well as Schlegelmilch 1982.

11 In this sense, even Klages mentions 'that, in the broad middle ground including the majority of the populace, the two groups of value orientations overlap, so that in the majority of people there is an *ambivalent presence and mixture* of conflicting values' (Klages and Kmeciak 1979: 342; emphasis in original).

12 This tangible threat to consciously perceived spaces for private action and decision-making seems to me to be where the spark is located which can ignite social conflicts and movements today (in contrast to lifeworlds defined by class culture). At least, it is possible from this position to understand the conditions setting such threats in motion, their topics and the logic of their progression. Thus, for instance, the very banal administrative act of a census can unleash a considerable social countermovement when it is perceived to be (or presented as) an uncontrollable infringement of personal privacy. Likewise, citizens' initiative groups and the like typically arise wherever bureaucratic decisions infringe privacy, which is experienced as something personally determined and determinable. In this sense the planned superhighway through one's own backyard, the nuclear power plant around the corner and the storage of nuclear weapons in densely populated Germany

also constitute an interference where people become aware of them as life-threatening risks, an interference that threatens their own existence directly, even physically, and thus creates the *new communal status of a 'shared hazard'* (on this, see below).

13   On this point and the subsequent discussion, cf. Beck-Gernsheim 1983.

14   This is a primary reason why, precisely under the conditions of individualization (which does after all imply that people are removed from the social assistance and support systems of neighbourhood and family), the actual or impending loss of a job is experienced as a particular threat. At the same time, this fundamental dependence on paid labour compels people almost automatically to adapt themselves to the expectations of others and supervisors, *contrary* to the emergence of a new values orientation. In this case, the new orientations are concealed behind a sales facade of docile willingness to work. This probably applies particularly to periods of high unemployment, whereas in periods of full employment, substantive desires for self-realization and involvement in work are more likely to be expressed.

15   In a summary analysis of roughly 35 surveys on desired work times, Margarete Landenberger reaches the conclusion that the most frequent wish is to lower the retirement age or make it more flexible, followed by a shortening of the working week and a lengthening of the annual vacation time. The important variables prove to be employment status, income, age, gender and the specific working conditions (Landenberger 1983).

16   See Beck, Brater and Daheim 1980, ch. 8.

17   For examples in the service sector, see Ingfer 1982.

18   Kern and Schumann 1983: 358; and even more clearly Kern and Schumann 1984.

19   Giarni and Lougergé 1978, as cited by Zapf 1983.

Chapter 7   Misunderstanding Reflexivity

1   The fact that the coordinates inside/outside (alongside inclusion/exclusion, secure/insecure (knowledge/unawareness) and political/unpolitical) are intended to describe and comprehend the conflict lines of second modernity is presented in chapter 2 above.

2   See ch. 1 above.

3   Reiss 1992; cf. also Bonss 1995.

4   Quotes from the German translation, *Strukturen der Lebenswelt*, vol. 1 (1979), pp. 214–17.

5   Wildavsky 1995: ch. 14. For extensive discussion of this point, cf. Beck 1996: 161ff., 'The art of doubt'.

6   This has been worked out, in particular, by Brian Wynn in numerous publications; cf. also Hajer 1995.

7   On the concept of 'countermodern', see Beck 1996: ch. 2.

8   On this point, see Heller 1994.

Chapter 10　How Neighbours Become Jews

1　'This was how it began – from the Nuremberg laws to the Jewish star. From
week to week since 1933 the special laws against Jews were intensified': a
documentation of the systematic deprivation of rights which all Germans
at that time had experienced was compiled by Armin von Manikowsky, in
Stern, no. 6, 1 Feb. 1979. See also the documentation in Rosenstrauch 1988.
2　'Unser Vater war Kameruner, unsere Mutter Ostpreußin, wir sind Mulattin-
nen. Die Schwestern Frieda P. und Anna G. erzählen aus ihrem Leben', in
Oguntoye et al. 1992: 84.
3　The definite article – the stranger or the strangers – is completely inappropriate; it negates the categorical indefiniteness of the concept.
4　This irritation is also expressed in the Latin term *hostis* which means both
enemy and guest.
5　This applies to the example of homosexuals and even more directly to
bisexuals.
6　This existential ambivalence is generalizable; it also determines the debate
between feminists and post-feminists, for example. What does femininity
mean? With the increasing equality of men and women, the clearness of
'being a woman' is forgotten. Perhaps 'ambivalence as existence' will become
a biographical characteristic of 'reflexive modernity' (more about that later).
7　I have been describing what 'manufactured uncertainty' means in publications since *Gegengifte* (Frankfurt, 1988; translated as *Ecological Politics in
the Age of Risk*, 1994), that is '(mega)threats', distinguished from 'risks'.
The concept of 'manufactured uncertainty' is broader; it relates not only to
technical developments, but also to economic upheavals and the erosion of
the welfare state, the political system and the bourgeois government of laws
and security. On this point, cf. Ewald 1993b; Bonss 1993; Giddens 1994.
8　The all-encompassing word *Unsicherheit* used in the original here confuses
two concepts which are separated for good reason in English as *unsafety*
and *insecurity*: the threat from unbridled violence and criminality, or the
loss of security due to the break-up of traditional lifestyles. The deliberate
dramatization of the decay of values and (organized) criminality is far from
the least important source of energy for neonationalism in Europe.
9　Translator's note: *Asylant* is a pejorative term for asylum applicants used
in contemporary German political discourse.
10　Translator's note: this refers to a long-time standard German handbook of
history.

Chapter 11　Nation-States without Enemies

1　'The internalized norms of civilization', writes Philipp Reemtsma (1992),
'exist . . . after all, to prevent the excesses of "hot" cruelty – but "cold
cruelty" does the same thing and even more, only "coldly". In "cold"

cruelty, civilization enlists its own rules for an attack on itself. It allies with itself against itself.'

2 For details on the debate over individualization see Beck and Beck-Gernsheim 1996; also ch. 3 above and the literature cited there in note 1.

3 Translator's note: this is the popular term for an edict of the German government from the 1970s which barred adherents of the German Communist Party and other (left-wing) extremists from the civil service.

Chapter 12 Brief Introduction to Environmental Machiavellianism

1 On the definition of nature and the misunderstandings and conflicts arising from it, see Beck 1994, esp. ch. 2.

References

Abels, H. 1993: *Jugend von der Moderne*, Opladen.

Albrow, M. 1996a: *The Global Age*, Cambridge.

—— 1996b: 'Travelling beyond local cultures: socioscapes in a global city', in John Eade (ed.), *Living in the Global City*, London.

Améry, J. 1977: *Jenseits von Schuld und Sühne*, Stuttgart.

Anderson, B. 1983: *Imagined Communities: the Origin and Spread of Nationalism*, London.

Arendt, H. 1958: 'Freiheit und Politik', *Neue Rundschau* 69, pp. 670–94.

—— 1979: *Eichmann in Jerusalem*, Harmondsworth.

Bahrdt, H. P. 1975: 'Erzählte Lebensgeschichten von Arbeitern', in M. Osterland (ed.), *Arbeitssituation, Lebenslage und Konfliktpotential*, Frankfurt.

Bauman, Z. 1990: *Thinking Sociologically*, Cambridge.

—— 1992: *Modernity and Ambivalence*, Cambridge.

—— 1996: 'Wir sind alle Vagabunden', *Süddeutsche Zeitung*, 10 Sept.

Beck, U. 1982: 'Folgeprobleme der Modernisierung und die Stellung der Soziologie in der Praxis', in U. Beck (ed.), *Soziologie und Praxis*, Special Issue 1 of *Soziale Welt*, Göttingen, pp. 1–23.

—— 1983: 'Jenseits von Stand und Klasse? Soziale Ungleichheiten, gesellschaftliche Individualisierungsprozesse und die Entstehung neuer sozialer Identitäten und Formationen', in R. Kreckel (ed.), *Soziale Ungleichheiten*, Special Issue 2 of *Soziale Welt*, Göttingen, pp. 35–74.

—— 1992: *Risk Society*, London.

—— 1993: *Die Erfindung des Politischen*, Frankfurt; trans. as *The Reinvention of Politics*, Cambridge, 1996.

—— 1994: *Ecological Politics in the Age of Risk*, Cambridge.

—— 1996: *The Reinvention of Politics*, Cambridge.

—— 1997a: 'Das Zeitalter der Gleichheit', in Beck 1997b.

—— (ed.) 1997b: *Kinder der Freiheit*, Frankfurt.

—— 1997c: *Was ist Globalisierung?*, Edition Zweite Moderne, Frankfurt.

Beck, U. and Beck-Gernsheim, E. 1995: *The Normal Chaos of Love*, Cambridge.

—— 1996: 'Individualization and "precarious freedoms"', in Heelas et al. 1996.

—— (eds) 1994: *Riskante Freiheiten*, Frankfurt.

Beck, U., Brater, M. and Daheim, H. 1980: *Soziologie der Arbeit und der Berufe*, Reinbeck.

Beck, U., Giddens, A. and Lash, S. 1994: *Reflexive Modernization*, Cambridge. Trans. into German as *Reflexive Modernisierung*, Frankfurt, 1996.

Beck-Gernsheim, E. 1983: 'Vom "Dasein für andere" zum Anspruch auf ein "Stück eigenes Leben"', *Soziale Welt*, no. 3.

—— 1994: 'Auf dem Wege in die postfamiliale Familie', in Beck and Beck-Gernsheim 1994.

Benn, G. 1986: *Das Gottfried Benn Brevier: Aphorismen, Reflexionen, Maximen und Briefen*, Munich.

—— 1989: *Essays und Reden* (Essays and speeches), Frankfurt.

Benseler, F., Heinze, R. G. and Klönne, A. 1982: *Zukunft der Arbeit*, Hamburg.

Berger, P. A. 1995: *Statusunsicherheit und Erfahrungsvielfalt: Sozialstrukturelle Individualisierungsprozesse und Fluktuationsdynamiken in der Bundesrepublik Deutschland*, Opladen.

Bonss, W. 1993: 'Unsicherheit als politisches Problem', *Mittelweg 36* (Feb.–Mar.)

—— 1995: *Vom Risiko. Unsicherheit und Ungewißheit in der Moderne*, Hamburg.

Dahrendorf, R. 1988: *The Modern Social Conflict: An Essay on the Politics of Liberty*, London.

Davis, M. 1992: 'Beyond *Blade Runner*: urban control. The ecology of fear', *Open Magazine*, no. 23.

Dettling, W. 1994: 'Und der Zukunft nicht zugewandt', *Die Zeit*, no. 30.

—— 1996: 'Was heißt Solidarität heute?', *Die Zeit*, 27 Dec.

Engfer, U., Hinrichs, K. and Wiesenthal, H. 1983: 'Arbeitswerte im Wandel', in Matthes 1983.

Enzensberger, H. M. 1991: *Mittelmaß und Wahn*, Frankfurt. Trans. as *Mediocrity and Delusion*, London, 1992.

Ewald, F. 1993a: *Der Versicherungsstaat*, Frankfurt.

—— 1993b: *Der Vorsorgestaat*, Frankfurt.

Fuchs, W. 1983: 'Jugendliche Statuspassage oder individualisierte Jugendbiographie?', *Soziale Welt*, no. 3.

Gellner, E. 1964: *Thought and Change*, London.

Gerhardt, U. 1990: *Gleichheit ohne Angleichung. Frauen im Recht*, Munich.

Giarni, O. and Lougergé, H. 1978: *The Diminishing Returns of Technology*, Oxford.

Giddens, A. 1990: *The Consequences of Modernity*, Cambridge.

—— 1991: *Self-Identity and Modernity*, Cambridge.

—— 1994: *Beyond Left and Right*, Cambridge.

Goffman, E. 1967: *Interaction Ritual*, New York.

Gore, A. 1992: *Earth in the Balance: Ecology and the Human Spirit*, Boston.

Hahn, A. 1994: 'Die soziale Konstruktion des Fremden', in W. M. Sprondel (ed.), *Die Objektivität der Ordnungen und ihre kommunikative Konstruktion*, Frankfurt.

Hajer, M. 1995: *The Politics of Environmental Discourse: Ecological Modernization and the Policy Process*, Oxford.

Heelas, P., Lash, S. and Morris, P. (eds) 1996: *De-traditionalization*, Oxford.

Heidegger, M. 1962: *Being and Time* (1927), London.

Heller, A. 1994: 'Die Zerstörung der Privatsphäre durch die Zivilgesellschaft', in Hitzler 1994.

Hesse, H. A. 1994: *Der Schutzstaat*, Baden-Baden.

Hirschmann, A. 1982: *Shifting Involvement: Private Interest and Public Action*, Princeton.

Hitzler, R. 1994: 'Mobilisierte Bürger', *Ästhetik und Kommunikation*, nos 85–6 (May).

—— 1996: 'Der alltägliche Machiavellismus', MS, Munich.

—— 1999: *Der gemeine Machiavellismus*, Frankfurt (forthcoming).

Hoffmann-Axhelm, D. 1993: *Die Dritte Stadt*, Frankfurt.

Hondrich, K.-O. 1994: 'Grenzen gegen die Gewalt', *Die Zeit*, 28 Jan., p. 4.

Hondrich, K.-O. and Koch-Arzberger, C. 1992: *Solidarität in der modernen Gesellschaft*, Frankfurt.

Ingfer, U. 1982: 'Arbeitszeitflexibilisierung als Rationalisierung', in H. Offe, K. Hinrichs and H. Wiesenthal (eds), *Arbeitszeitpolitik*, Frankfurt, pp. 106–15.

Inglehart, R. 1977: *The Silent Revolution: Changing Values and Political Styles among Western Publics*, Princeton.

Jagodzinski, W. 1983: 'Die zu stille Revolution', MS, Cologne.

Kant, I. 1983: *Perpetual Peace and Other Essays on Politics, History and Morality*, Cambridge.

Kern, H. and Schumann, M. 1983: 'Arbeit und Sozialcharakter: Alte und neue Konturen', in Matthes 1983.

—— 1984: 'Rationalisierung und Arbeiterbewußtsein', *Soziale Welt*, nos 1–2, pp. 146–58.

Kerr, C. 1979: 'The great American cultural evolution in the labor force', in Kerr and Rostow 1979.

Kerr, C. and Rostow, W. (eds) 1979: *Work in America: The Decade Ahead*, New York.

Keupp, H. 1995: 'Solidarisch und doch frei – für eine kommunitäre Individualität', *Psychologie Heute*, no. 7.

Klages, H. 1983: 'Wertwandel und Gesellschaftskrise in der sozialstaatlichen Demokratie', in Matthes 1983.

—— 1996: 'Der schwierige Bürger', in W. Weidenfeld (ed.), *Demokratie am Wendepunkt*, Berlin.

Klages, H. and P. Kmeciak (eds) 1979: *Wertwandel und gesellschaftlicher Wandel*, Frankfurt.

Köhler, G. and Meyer, M. (eds) 1994: *Die Folgen von 1989*, Munich.

Koolhaas, R. 1993: 'Die Entfaltung der Architektur', *ARCH: Zeitschrift für Architektur und Städtebau* 117 (June).

Kudera, S. 1982: *Das Bewußtsein der Deutschen: Empirische Ergebnisse und arbeitssoziologische Argumente zu einigen Klischees der Meinungs- und Werteforschung*, Munich.

Landenberger, M. 1983: *Arbeitszeitwünsche: Vergleichende Analyse vorliegender Befragungsergebnisse: Diskussionspapier des Wissenschaftszentrums Berlin*, Berlin.

Landmann, M. 1978: 'Mein Judentum', in H. J. Schultz (ed.), *Mein Judentum*, Munich.

Lash, S. and Urry, J. 1994: *Economies of Sign and Space*, London.

Lübbe, H. 1994: 'Wider die falschen Sorgen', in Köhler and Meyer 1994.

Mann, M. 1984: 'Capitalism and militarism', in M. Shaw (ed.), *War, State and Society*, New York.

Matthes, J. (ed.) 1983: *Krise der Arbeitsgesellschaft?*, Frankfurt.

—— 1992: *Zwischen den Kulturen?*, Göttingen.

Mönninger, M. 1993: 'Die dritte Heimat', *Frankfurter Allgemeine Zeitung*, 23 June, p. 29.

Mooser, J. 1983: 'Auflösung des proletarischen Milieus', *Soziale Welt*, no. 3.

Neckel, S. 1994a: 'Gefährliche Fremdheit', *Ästhetik und Kommunikation*, nos 85–6 (May).

—— 1994b: 'Politische Ethnizität', MS, Berlin.

Nietzsche, F. 1954: *Thus Spoke Zarathrustra*, Part 3, 'On passing by', in W. Kaufmann (ed. and trans.), *The Portable Nietzsche*, New York.

Offe, C. 1969: 'Politische Herrschaft und Klassenstrukturen', in G. Kress and D. Senghaas (eds), *Politikwissensschaft*, Frankfurt, pp. 155–89.

Oguntoye, K. et al. 1992: *Farbe bekennen*, Frankfurt. In English as *Showing our Colours*, London, 1992.

Olk, T. 1985: 'Jugend und gesellschaftliche Differenzierung', *Zeitschrift für Pädagogik (Beiheft)*.

Orfali, K. 1993: 'Modell der Transparenz: die schwedische Gesellschaft', in P. Ariès and G. Duby, *Die Geschichte des privaten Lebens. Vom Ersten Weltkrieg zur Gegenwart*, vol. 5, Frankfurt.

Prantl, H. 1994: 'Es wird ungesund in Deutschland', *Süddeutsche Zeitung*, 13–14 Aug., weekend supplement, p. V2/27.

Prittwitz, V. von 1990: *Das Katastrophen-Paradox*, Opladen.

Reemtsma, P. 1992: 'Vergangenheit als Prolog', *Mittelweg* 39/3, p. 22.

Reich, R. B. 1993: *Die neue Weltwirtschaft. Das Ende der nationalen Ökonomie*, Frankfurt.

Reiss, A. J. 1992: 'The institutionalization of risk', in Short and Clarke 1992.

Rosenstrauch, H. 1988: *Aus Nachbarn wurden Juden*, Berlin.

Sartre, J.-P. 1974: *Marxismus und Existentialismus*, Reinbeck.

Schlegelmilch, C. 1982: 'Grauer Arbeitsmarkt für Hochschulabsolventen', *Soziale Welt*, nos 3–4, pp. 400–30.

Schütz, A. and Luckmann, T. 1973: *The Structures of the Lifeworld*, vol. 1, Evanston, Ill.

Schütz, R. 1992: 'Die Stadt als Wahrnehmungsform', MS, Essen.

Shaw, M. 1988: *The Dialectics of War*, London.

Short, J. F. and Clarke, L. (eds), *Organizations, Uncertainties and Risk*, Boulder, Colo.

Simmel, G. 1950: 'The stranger', in *The Sociology of Georg Simmel*, trans. Kurt H. Wolff, New York.

Thompson, E. P. 1963: *The Making of the English Working Class*, London.

Tocqueville, A. de 1945: *Democracy in America*, New York.

Tucholsky, K. 1985: 'Berliner Geselligkeiten', in Tucholsky, *Gesammelte Werke: Ergänzungsband 1911–1928*, Hamburg.

Vester, M. 1970: *Die Entstehung des Proletariats als Lernprozeß*, Frankfurt.

Wette, W. 1993: 'Kein Kind der Demokratie: Zur geplanten Verkleinerung der Bundeswehr: Ein Plädoyer gegen die Wehrpflicht', *Die Zeit*, 19 Feb., p. 5.

Wiedenroth, E. 1992: 'Was macht mich so anders in den Augen der Anderen?', in Oguntoye 1992.

Wildavsky, A. 1995: *But Is It True? A Citizen's Guide to Environmental Health and Safety Issues*, Cambridge, Mass.

Wilkinson, H. 1997: 'Kinder der Freiheit', in Beck 1997b.

Wilkinson, H. and Mulgan, G. 1995: *Freedom's Children*, London.

Wong, D. 1992: 'Fremdheitsfiguren im gesellschaftlichen Diskurs', in Matthes 1992.

Wuthnow, R. 1997: 'Active compassion', in Beck 1997b.

Yankelovich, D. 1979: 'Work, values, and the new breed', in Kerr and Rostow 1979.

—— 1994: 'Wohlstand und Wertewandel – das Ende der fetten Jahre (Auszug aus einem Report für die Clinton-Administration)', *Psychologie Heute*, no. 3.

Zapf, W. 1983: 'Entwicklungsdilemma und Innovationspotentiale in modernen Gesellschaften', in Matthes 1983.

Zoelick, R. 1993: 'Stärker nach Osten blicken. Welche Rolle soll die Bundesrepublik in der Welt spielen? Ein Amerikaner rät den Deutschen, ihre außenpolitische Position neu zu bestimmen', *Die Zeit*, 26 Nov., p. 10.

Index

Index by Zeb Korycinska